Then the king will say to those at his right hand, "Come, you who are blessed by my Father, inherit the kingdom prepared for you from the foundation of the world, for I was hungry and you gave me food, I was thirsty and you gave me something to drink, I was a stranger and you welcomed me, I was naked and you gave me clothing, I was sick and you took care of me, I was in prison and you visited me." Then the righteous will answer him, "Lord, when was it that we saw you hungry and gave you food or thirsty and gave you something to drink? And when was it that we saw you a stranger and welcomed you or naked and gave you clothing? And when was it that we saw you sick or in prison and visited you?" And the king will answer them, "Truly I tell you, just as you did it to one of the least of these brothers and sisters of mine, you did it to me."

Matthew 25:34-40 (NRSV)

Testimonials

Bishop Ken Carder is the consummate storyteller. These stories of his life will draw you into the broader narrative where you will not only be with Ken as he is living on the margins of society, but you will find out that the margins are God's favorite place to hang out as well. Ken is, time and time again, a means of grace as he lays witness to one resurrection after another.

May you live into his stories and allow them to shape a new path for you as they paved a new way of being in the world for me.

Cari Willis
Chaplain to those on death row

In *Shifting Margins,* Bishop Ken Carder recounts his early life and the trials and joys of growing up poor in southern Appalachia. He shares family stories of those whose religion and family values buttressed and sustained them. Equally important, he shares very personal and intimate experiences as a pastor and bishop in an era filled with racial strife, helping him realize his privilege and the injustice that prejudices leave in their wake.

It is a memoir of God's faithfulness toward a preacher whose integrity, patience, and love for family, the church, and the penitent remind us of the divine grace that abounds in the places, spaces, and faces we encounter and experience daily.

Read, laugh, and cry. Be encouraged. Then go and do likewise.

Robin Dease
Bishop, North Georgia Conference of The United Methodist Church

Ken Carder's gentle storytelling reflects the heart of a sage. His childhood of poverty, adulthood of privilege and power, and deep reflection about systemic oppression draw the reader into the complexities and beauty of humanity. The stitching together of transformative experiences becomes the literary patchwork quilt of love. Wrapping the reader in hope and centering people on the margins, Carder appropriates a lifetime of storied wisdom as a gift to be opened.

Connie Mitchell Shelton
Bishop, North Carolina Conference of The United Methodist Church

Shifting Margins is the story of growing up in the Appalachian hills of East Tennessee. Bishop Carder's book is a lesson in the lived experience of poverty, marginalization, and powerlessness. Even a naïve person of privilege will be exposed to a significant index of how to begin relationships with the poor and the oppressed by simply walking through these pages. It is also the story of Carder's pastoral ministry and episcopacy—the challenges, issues, failures he had to confront, and the victories he knew. Do yourself a favor: walk with this poor kid, preacher, pastor, professor, and episcopal leader through the last eighty years. It will inform, and it may transform your life.

Tex Sample
Robert B. And Kathleen Rogers Professor Emeritus of Church and Society, Saint Paul School of Theology

Stories disclose, shape, and transform the storyteller and the hearer. Bishop Ken Carder is a gifted and generous storyteller. Ken tells his story with clarity, sensitivity, vulnerability, and grace. In so doing, he connects us not just to himself but to our humanity and to the God who longs for God's story to become fully alive in each of us and all of us. I am so glad Megan kept saying, "Pawpaw, tell me a story."

Gregory V. Palmer
Bishop, Ohio West Area, The United Methodist Church

Bishop Carder's memoir witnesses to the spiritual growth possible when a Christian reflects on the shifting margins around them. The story models the kind of reevaluation possible when a faithful person encounters dissonance in religion, economics, race relations, incarceration, and health—and leans into learning from it. Each chapter draws the reader into increased engagement and intimacy with the situations Bishop Carder has faced. *Shifting Margins* is a must-read for any person interested in spiritual formation.

Pamela Couture
Emeritus Professor of Church and Community,
Emmanuel College of Victoria University in the University of Toronto

SHIFTING MARGINS

From Fear and Exclusion
Toward Love and Belonging

Bishop Kenneth L. Carder

Market Square
BOOKS

SHIFTING MARGINS
From Fear and Exclusion Toward Love and Belonging

©2024 Kenneth Carder
books@marketsquarebooks.com
141 N. Martinwood, Suite 2 Knoxville, Tennessee 37923

ISBN: 978-1-950899-83-8

Printed and Bound in the United States of America
Cover Illustration & Book Design ©2024 Market Square Publishing, LLC

Editor: Sheri Carder Hood
Post-Process Editor: Ken Rochelle
Page Design: Carrie Rood
Cover Design: Kevin Slimp

All rights reserved. No part of this book may be reproduced in any manner without written permission except in the case of brief quotations included in critical articles and reviews. For information, please contact Market Square Publishing, LLC.

Scripture quotations used with permission from:

NRSV
New Revised Standard Version Bible, copyright © 1989 National Council of the Churches of Christ in the United States of America.
Used by permission. All rights reserved worldwide.

Contents

Acknowledgments 1

Introduction 3

Part 1 – Formation 7

    Chapter One: Birthed and Nurtured on the Margins 9

    Chapter Two: Early Movements from Poverty to Privilege 25

    Chapter Three: A Whole New World and a Radical Shift 51

    Chapter Four: Transitioning Back Home and a Changed World 75

Part 2 - Ministry With Those on the Margins 81

    Chapter Five: Poverty, Privilege, and Ministry 83

    Chapter Six: Confrontation with Personal and Institutional Racism 119

    Chapter Seven: "I Was in Prison …" 155

    Chapter Eight: Dementia and Diminishment:
        Gifts from the Forgetting and the Forgotten 187

Part 3 - Conclusion 217

    Chapter Nine: Margins Keep Shifting 219

Acknowledgments

Adequately acknowledging the people who made the book possible is impossible. Most remain anonymous, and many have joined that "great cloud of witnesses" whose memories continue to cheer me on. I'm grateful to those who felt I had something worthwhile to share. Among them are colleagues and friends, including Mary McClintock Fulkerson, with whom I co-taught a course at Duke on "Shaping Communities of Justice"; Peter Storey, whose friendship and courageous leadership have challenged and inspired me for more than thirty years; Tex Sample, whose presence with and organizing among "hard-living people" has provided rich conversations across decades; and Karl Netting, a personal and pastoral confidante with whom I share a special bond forged across fifty years.

Enthusiastic encouragement has come from my family, particularly my daughters, Sandra Nash and Sheri Hood, their families, and my wife, Norma Sessions. Granddaughter Megan Hood started the whole idea with her childhood prodding, "Pawpaw, tell me a story." My other grandkids—Katelyn Nash Aiken, Emily and Michael Nash, and Julia Rose Hood—added their inspiration. Kevin Slimp of Market Square Books graciously invited me to submit the manuscript for publication and gently prodded me to complete it. A special thanks to my editor, Sheri Carder Hood, who has been the most persistent encourager, helpful critic, and creative partner in the writing process. She was more than a detached editor. As my daughter, she contributed empathetic knowledge of many experiences and relationships chronicled in the stories.

Those most responsible for the book, however, are the people of southern Appalachia with whom I share a common culture. Growing up on the margins of a marginalized region of the country prepared me for a lifetime of friendship and ministry with people on society's edges. They have been, and continue to be, my kinfolk, my colleagues, and my inspiration. They are a primary means of God's loving presence and transforming power. It is among those on the margins—the poor, the oppressed, the imprisoned, the sick, the vulnerable—that we meet and serve God, as Jesus declares: "… just as you did it to one of the least of these who are members of my family, you did it to me" (Matthew 25:40).

Introduction

Where, oh where is pretty (sweet) little Susie?
Where, oh where is pretty little Susie?
Where, oh where is pretty little Susie?
Way down yonder in the paw-paw patch.

I learned it early. It's a popular folk song in southern Appalachia, the place that birthed and shaped me. Many who are well acquainted with the lyrics and tune have no idea what a pawpaw is. After all, "Pawpaw" is a familiar name given to one's grandfather, especially in the South. My grandchildren call me "Pawpaw."

During the Great Depression, the pawpaw was widely consumed as a substitute for more expensive fruits. It's loaded with nutrients equal to or surpassing apples, oranges, and bananas. The pawpaw—often called the "poor man's banana," "hillbilly banana," or "hillbilly mango"—was marginalized in the food world after the Great Depression. It became associated with Appalachian culture, stereotypically characterized by poverty and ignorance by the mid-twentieth century and considered "uncultured." In a sense, the pawpaw is a metaphor for marginalization.

Pawpaw groves, with their interconnected roots and nutritious fruits, reflect my own experience as the son of Appalachian tenant farmers, textile mill workers, and hard-living people of the land. Underneath the visible pawpaw trees are interwoven, intertwined roots clinging together to share life-giving nutrients. From one taproot, an intricate colony of subterranean root sprouts can emerge, creating a visible community of flourishing trees. I owe much to my Appalachian roots and the interwoven fabric of my native culture. I am the product of its richness and its poverty, its beauty and its blight, its promise and its peril, its privileges and its prejudices, its anguish and its hopes.

As a child, our granddaughter Megan would climb onto my lap or snuggle beside me and say, "Pawpaw, tell me a story." After exhausting my repertoire of children's stories, I reached into memories of my own childhood to entertain her. Those stories became her favorites. During a visit when she was four years old, I was awakened early one morning by the sound of Megan skipping up the hallway. As she neared my room, she began singing:

> *Where, oh where is sweet little Pawpaw?*
> *Where, oh where is sweet little Pawpaw?*
> *Where, oh where is sweet little Pawpaw?*
> *Way down yonder in the paw-paw patch!*

Thereafter, my stories were known as "Stories from the Pawpaw Patch." What follows are reflections on experiences and relationships that formed me, taught me, challenged me, saddened me, and gave me hope. They are stories from the margins where I have encountered the God who persistently shifts boundaries and includes the vulnerable, the poor, the powerless, and the pushed-aside at the center of divine presence and purpose.

Writing this book has been a struggle. It feels presumptuous to assume my experiences are of interest or value to others outside my immediate family and close friends. Yet, every person's life has unique significance, and it is through sharing our stories that we discover and contribute to our common humanity. Several friends and colleagues familiar with my personal and vocational journey across multiple boundaries have insisted my story might help others broaden their own stories. My intent is to highlight the lessons I have learned from those on society's margins.

Reflecting on the past is painful. Letting go of sins, mistakes, failures, regrets, grief, and guilt is hard. I've learned that preaching and teaching about grace comes easier for me than accepting grace and forgiveness for myself. Writing this book included a lot of silent confessions as painful memories surfaced beyond those in the manuscript.

Another struggle is evident in the book's organization and structure. The tension has been creating coherence between chronology and core themes. Initial drafts followed a simple chronology of events and experiences.

However, it seemed more coherent to structure the stories around the central theme related to marginalization by dividing the book into three sections. Section One focuses on my formation among the marginalized. Section Two focuses on ministry amid societal challenges of economic disparity, racism, prisons and criminal justice, and ageism and dementia. Section Three concludes with the challenges of moving forward.

The topics selected for inclusion have been in the forefront of my six decades of ordained ministry. However, margins in perceptions, understandings, and relationships are constantly being realigned and expanded as events unfold. Current controversies around human sexuality, abortion, political polarization, authoritarianism, and religious and political extremism are but a few of the areas in which boundaries are shifting. What lessons do we need to learn from those marginalized by such controversies and realities? I hope the following stories will be helpful as the margins continue to shift.

Part I

FORMATION

CHAPTER ONE

Birthed and Nurtured on the Margins

Born and Raised in Poverty

Into the "pawpaw patch" of southern Appalachia, I was born November 18, 1940, the fourth of six children of Allen and Edith Walker Carder. The devastation of poverty, accompanied by inadequate medical care, had already set a tone in our house. Mom and Dad knew the grief of losing a child as their firstborn, David, died at age two from diphtheria. My sister, Edna, barely survived the same illness. Mom and Dad married early, at ages sixteen and eighteen, respectively.

My first four years were lived in a small rental house near the railroad tracks in Washington County, Tennessee, within walking distance of my maternal grandparents. Watching and waving at the passing freight and passenger trains was a favorite pastime. The passenger trains were often crowded with soldiers on their way to or from the "great war."

Dad worked long hours at the nearby textile plant. He

received his draft notice and was ordered to report for induction into the Army. Two uncles were already serving overseas. Dad packed his belongings and prepared to leave. Much to the surprise of our household, he got notice just before departing for the train station that he did not have to report. His work was considered vital to the war effort, and he was deferred. What a relief!

In 1944, Dad's doctor advised him to move to a drier climate for health reasons. At one point, he contracted tuberculosis and often experienced shortness of breath, hoarseness, and severe coughs. Dad smoked, but smoking was not yet associated with health problems. So Dad headed for Laredo, Texas, leaving us behind until he could find a job. Shortly after that, Mom sold all our meager household belongings and prepared to move to Texas, although Dad had not yet found employment. Granddaddy Walker accompanied us to help Mom take care of four kids, the youngest only eighteen months old. After all, it was a trip of almost 1,500 miles! The soldiers on board teased me and called me "Red." My red hair, inherited from my maternal grandmother, made me stand out among my siblings. It sometimes sparked cynical questions when the family appeared together: "Well, where did he get that red hair?" Dad would retort, "It come with his head!"

We arrived in Laredo in late January. The contrast between the mountains and hills of eastern Tennessee and the dry flatland of Texas was stark, even to a five-year-old. It was my first encounter with anyone who was a different color and spoke a different language. We frequently walked across the river into Mexico to buy sugar, which was rationed in the U.S.

Unable to find work, Dad and Mom decided, "We don't belong here. Let's go home." So, we packed our few belongings, boarded the train, and returned to Washington County. We had no furniture, no car, a few clothes in suitcases, and no money. We were among the desperately poor, with only an extended family to provide help, primarily Granddaddy and Granny Walker. Thankfully, the textile mill offered Dad his old job, working the second shift from four p.m. until midnight six days each week.

Working the later shift left the mornings and afternoons free for other work. Granddaddy was a subsistence farmer who did odd jobs for pay. He and Dad decided our family's best opportunity for housing was as tenant farmers. So, we moved into a little two-room, clapboard shack on a farm on Knob Creek Road. The house barely shielded us from the wind and cold. Light penetrated the cracks in the walls. Rain fell through the leaking roof and was caught in buckets. There was no indoor plumbing, running water, or electricity. The floor was rough wood with open spaces to the dirt beneath. The house sat beside a main road where cars passed on the way to Johnson City.

A car stopped one morning as I was playing in a mud puddle near the road. The woman rolled down her window and asked, "Are you hungry?" I didn't understand the question. I was not hungry since we always had food—mostly pinto beans, vegetables from the garden, eggs from the chickens roaming near the house, and milk from the cows. Something about the tone of her voice or the look in her eyes made me uncomfortable. I felt different, lacking, less than, looked down upon. It may have been the first time I was conscious of being marginalized.

Dangled over a Rain Barrel

It was an early morning in May 1945. The surrounding alfalfa field had been freshly mowed. The birds were singing, a rooster crowed in the distance, and the cows' mooing could be heard from the barn down the road. I had climbed upon the small tool shed nearby. With a stick as a pretend hammer, I banged on the tin roof. I was lost in an imaginary adult world of useful work, glancing back occasionally toward the unpainted house that was home to my mom, dad, two brothers, Jim and Dennis, and our sister, Edna. Dad was still asleep, having worked the second shift at the mill. I tried not to hammer too hard and wake him up because he was grumpy when he didn't get his sleep.

Suddenly, my imaginary world was shattered by a shrill command: "Get off that building, you red-headed brat!" As the landlord walked toward the tool shed, I jumped to the ground and ran into the house. My mother quietly hugged me and shut the squeaking door without speaking to the angry landowner. After all, you don't "bite the hand that feeds you" or challenge the behavior of the one on whom you were dependent. Tenant farming was a prevalent way of life for many in rural Appalachia in the

1940s and 1950s, and it had been the dominant lot of the Carder and Walker clans for generations.

Dad left for his job at the textile mill around three in the afternoon that memorable day. Mom gathered the four kids and took us to play in the yard outside the big white house up the hill. There, she cleaned and ironed for the landlord's family. Edna was nine, Jim was seven, Dennis was two, and I was in the middle. We played quietly in the yard, hoping to be unnoticed by the "big man." But from around the corner of the two-story farmhouse drunkenly staggered the one who scared me a few hours earlier. Upon spotting me, he yelled, "You're the kid that was on my building. I'm going to teach you a lesson!"

He grabbed me tightly and dragged me toward the rain barrel full of water from the spring showers. He picked me up by my heels, hoisted me above the rainwater, and said, "I'm going to drown you. You will respect my property." I was too scared to cry, but Jim and Edna began to scream. My mother emerged from the house. With fear and trembling, she begged him to leave me alone. He laughed as though her protests only added to his sport. Soon, however, his wife came to my aid, grabbed him around the waist, and said, "Leave the boy alone." He dropped me beside the rain barrel and staggered away laughing.

Thereafter, he boasted about teaching me to respect him and his property. Yes, I did stay off his buildings. I dutifully addressed him as "sir." The slightest gesture from him received a "Thank you, sir." But respect him? I loathed him, despised him, was terrified of him! My dad, who had a temper, was furious when he heard about the incident. But rather than confront the landowner, he made plans to move to another farm. He didn't want to be labeled a troublemaker by the other farmers in the area, so he quietly sought another place to rent. We moved to a larger and better house up the road, still within view and walking distance of that big white house, now a clear sign of wealth, power, and abuse!

School started for me in September 1945. Edna, Jim, and I walked to Oak Hill, a one-room schoolhouse. We were all in the same room. With no running water, we all drank from a bucket that held water from the spring nearby.

Though I wasn't aware then, being held over a rain barrel was the dramatic beginning of a lifelong personal grappling with the tension between economics and power, wealth and privilege, and having and being. The pervasive influence of economics and market capitalism is inescapable and manifests itself in both subtle and dramatic ways. Living with that tension has been part of my journey from poverty to privilege, from powerlessness to positions of power, from preoccupation with achieving to a focus on authentic *being* as a child of God. Fortunately, the experience of powerlessness and exploitation of being dangled over a rain barrel by an intoxicated landlord was balanced early by a different expression of power and wealth.

In late December, we moved again, about two miles away from the site of the rain barrel incident. The owner,

Mr. Street, lived across the mountain in Buladean, North Carolina. This tenant house was more adequate—four rooms, well-kept, beside a creek and amid rolling hills. Mr. Street was seldom present, but when he did visit, he brought pockets full of candy for us kids. When I saw his pickup truck coming, I ran toward the road, climbed the gate, and eagerly greeted him. He would rub my red hair playfully and say, "You red-headed brat." The same words used by the one who terrorized me were now words of affection and laughter rather than anger and threat!

It was on the Street farm that I remember working in the fields. I hoed corn alongside my mom, dad, granddad, Jim, and Edna. I helped feed the chickens and pigs. Mom worked the fields with us in the summer while, at the same time, cooking our meals on a wood stove, washing clothes in a tub, wringing them out by hand, and hanging them on the clothesline. Dad continued his grueling work schedule—in the fields until noon and then to the textile mill until midnight. We never went on "vacation," and Dad seldom took a day off. An "outing" was a drive to visit relatives.

Mr. Street gave a young boy a needed counter-image of wealth and power. He treated us with respect, even alerting us by mail before visiting. He joined beside us in the fields. I never felt afraid or intimidated in his presence. I learned later that he even encouraged my dad to buy his own little farm and offered to help secure the money. He was more about empowering than domination. We grieved when the news came that he had been killed in a tragic accident on his farm in North Carolina.

From this house, we kids caught the bus to Boones Creek Elementary School. We now had separate rooms for each grade, running water, water fountains, and indoor toilets. As I learned to read, I began to like school and no longer pretended to be sick as an excuse to stay home. Although education was not emphasized and the Bible was the only book in our home, school and learning became a means of compensating for my feelings of inferiority and the stigma of being poor.

A Scary God and a Religion of Fear

Being dangled over a rain barrel as punishment and as a lesson in respect for one with power had its counterpart in an unexpected place: church. We attended an independent Baptist church pastored by my dad's cousin. He was a "shouting" preacher with an elementary school education. He vividly described human beings as sinners worthy of eternal damnation in a burning lake of fire. God was the creator and righteous judge to whom we owed our loyalty and obedience. God despised sin, and we were all sinners!

Though I was too young for the most often mentioned sins—cheatin', gamblin', drinkin', dancin', playin' cards, cussin', carousin', stealin'—the preacher made it clear that we "are born in sin" and "ain't worthy of God's favor." We deserve "eternal damnation in hell." But, he'd say God has provided an escape. God sent his son, Jesus, to die for our sins, and if we accept Jesus as our Savior, we could be spared from "the lake of fire." Although that preacher had likely never heard of Jonathan Edwards or "total depravity," he had Edwards' gift for creating fear and trembling.

In addition to that small Baptist church, we attended revivals, camp meetings, and crusades. There, we heard the traveling evangelists and faith healers whose messages were apocalyptic and pre-millennial. These were the waning days of World War II, and Revelation, Daniel, and the "little apocalypse" of Matthew and Mark were favorite texts. The signs of the times with wars and rumors of wars pointed to an imminent end and the beginning of the "great tribulation." The rapture was near, and being left behind to "the weeping and wailing and gnashing of teeth" was the dreaded fear that kept me awake many nights.

Among the preachers heard was Mordicai F. Hamm, under whose ministry Billy Graham was converted. I heard him talk about the "mark of the beast" and "prove" the identity of the anti-Christ. His preaching scared me. Though more educated and sophisticated than the shouting preacher, Hamm's message was one of impending doom. Fear as motivation for "accepting Jesus" permeated his preaching. The message was fatalistic, with the only hope being "going to heaven" when we die. He and our preacher at the Baptist church spoke angrily about "infidels" and "modernist" preachers who didn't believe in the Bible. I saw one preacher burn a copy of the "new Bible" translated by the "infidels" and "Communists," referring to the *Revised Standard Version*. Ironically, I often imitated those preachers while roaming the fields by mounting stumps and calling the surrounding weeds and trees to repent.

The threat of hell and an impending catastrophic end to the world, with my parents being taken away in a rapture, shaped my worldview and image of God. Coupled with the vivid memory of being held over a rain barrel for wrongs committed against one with wealth and power, religion reinforced feelings of worthlessness and insecurity. Strangely, however, the certainty of dogmatic religion and black-and-white morality provided a twisted sense of hope. The way to a secure future was acquiescing to the belief system of fundamentalism and "accepting Jesus as my Savior." Then, I would go to heaven and escape the "great tribulation" and eternal damnation.

Admittedly, those formative years as tenant farmers and being part of a fear-based, dogmatic, rigid religion had lifelong consequences. It has not been easy to trust and love God. A deep sense of inferiority and of not measuring up dog me to this day. Fear of failure spawns a perfectionistic streak, which makes self-acceptance rooted in grace more easily preached and taught than accepted for me. The tension between law and gospel has been my constant companion since childhood. Images of God as a strict judge and loving parent have competed for dominance in my personal journey.

Fortunately, other persons and communities countered the harsh images and experiences. My parents and extended family embodied love, boundless compassion, gentle courage, and strong resilience. My dad's hard work and constant pressure to provide the family with basic shelter, food, and clothing left little energy for calm and laughter. His irritability and occasional outbursts of anger frequently created tension, and he was not prone to show affection to the kids. However, my mother's calm demeanor and tender affection and my grandfather's tranquil, humble spirit more than compensated for Dad's emotional distance. Granddaddy Walker worked the farms with us, and he never seemed to lose patience with rowdy kids eager to leave the cornfield or tobacco patch for a game of marbles or hide-and-seek.

Granny Walker was more outwardly pious than her husband, though kind and affectionate. She had taught Sunday School at McKinley Methodist Church when my mom was growing up. She left the Methodist church when, as she said, "The Methodists stopped shouting." She was more at home in the Pentecostal church nearby. I accompanied her several times. The people were warm and friendly, unlike what I experienced in the independent Baptist church, and I wasn't scared by the preacher's sermons. The shouting was done mostly by the women, including Granny. It seemed to make her happy! Mom was much more reserved than her mother, and she never became emotional in church.

The Pentecostal services were emotional, but the emotion wasn't one of fear. Happiness and joy dominated. When the preacher got excited, his cadence of speech changed from deliberate to words jumbled together. Sometimes, he would slip into "speaking in tongues," which triggered shouting and dancing in the aisles. While it all seemed strange, I was more fascinated than fearful, more curious than upset. Though the emphasis was on "going to heaven," it was more an anticipation of "going home" and "enjoying the streets of gold" and "pearly gates" than avoiding hell. Images of the afterlife made the drabness and suffering of this life temporary and bearable.

New Life on McKinley Road

Shortly after Mr. Street's death, we moved again. I was beginning the third grade. This move was different. My parents were excited. Dad took Mr. Street's advice and bought his own small farm on McKinley Road. It was across the railroad tracks from Granddaddy and Granny, and Mom's sister and her family lived within sight.

The house had three rooms and was in very poor condition. Green tarpaper shingles covering thin wooden planks separated us from the cold. There was no indoor plumbing or electricity. Across the hill was a pond, a barn, and a tool shed. The fifteen acres included rolling hills, a sinkhole filled with discarded trash and rats, a patch of woods, open spaces for pasture, a garden, corn, hay, and a plot for raising an allotment of tobacco. The tobacco provided needed money since Dad's job at the mill didn't pay enough to support a family of six. With Granddaddy Walker's help and a loan from a friend of Dad's, we soon had a cow, a pig, and chickens.

We were still poor, but it was different. My parents—especially Dad—felt more confident. He owned his "own place." Granddaddy, though illiterate, knew farming and how to make things grow. He had two horses we used to plow and cultivate the land. He taught me to ride and care for the horses, milk the cow, plow the fields, sucker and hoe tobacco, pick corn and beans, dig for potatoes, and stack hay in the barn. From age eight until I was a junior in high school, my summers were spent working on that small farm and hiring out to other farmers in the area.

I was always glad when school started because it was a break from the physical work in the field. When my granddaddy learned years later that I was going to be a Methodist preacher, he laughingly remarked, "I always knew you would do something that don't take much work!" Work, to him and my parents, meant physical labor! The Protestant work ethic was very much alive in the Carder home.

The holiness streak in my grandmother's faith and the rigid rules of Baptist morality influenced our leisure activities. Movies were forbidden, and no dancing or card games were allowed. Country music played on the radio. Games of hide-and-seek, kick-the-can, marbles, and baseball filled the few idle hours. We mostly played among ourselves and with cousins.

My favorite parts of the day were early morning and late evening. I walked the pasture alone to find the milk cow roaming through the patch of woods to the open field. There, I would dream of what life was like beyond McKinley Road and the hills of eastern Tennessee. I had glimpsed another world in the early trip to Texas, but those memories were fleeting. I was shy and dogged by feelings of inferiority. I grew increasingly embarrassed that our house didn't measure up to others in the neighborhood. Neighborhood kids had more stuff and didn't have to work as we did. They went on vacation and to the movies. Their parents drove nicer cars and bought new clothes. They had indoor plumbing and conveniences we lacked. Feelings of envy and resentment crept in. My complaints to Mom and Dad were met with both hurt and reprimand: "Be thankful for what you've got!" "We're doing the best we can." "You're too proud!"

School sparked my imagination and was where I felt affirmed by teachers. We walked the one mile to and from Midway School when the weather permitted and rode the school bus otherwise. Bullying was not uncommon, especially for new students. Jim, Edna, and I faced ridicule and occasional physical threats. Dad had cautioned us to "take care of one another and don't let anybody push you around." He warned, "Don't you ever start any fights, but if anybody jumps on you, fight back until it's over."

At the mill, Dad operated a large machine he called the "slasher." I'm still unsure what it did with the yarn, but it required skill and attentiveness. The temperatures often reached a hundred degrees in his workspace. He was diligent, dependable, and hardworking. His supervisors respected him, but he would sometimes poke fun at them, especially the young ones with college degrees. He often smirked at "their book learning, but they don't know nothin' about a slasher!"

Granddaddy Walker's quiet dignity and calm self-respect were expressed differently. I never heard him boast or "cuss" or even express verbal anger at anyone. Mom told me about an incident that characterized his response to being treated without respect. Since the only money he made was from plowing gardens, selling tobacco in the fall, and doing other manual jobs for neighbors, he had difficulty paying bills. Mom and Dad persuaded him to apply for "welfare."

He went reluctantly to the courthouse to apply. When it came time to sign the forms, he admitted he couldn't write. The insensitive staff member mockingly exclaimed, "You mean you can't even sign your name?" As Mom told the story, Granddaddy, a tall and handsome man, rose steadily from his chair, stared intensely at the stunned social worker, and firmly said, "Come on, Edith, let's go! I'll starve before I accept anything from them." He walked out of the office, perhaps teaching the startled woman a lesson: being treated with dignity is a basic human need. "You ain't no better than anyone else, but you ain't less either," was Granddaddy's familiar mantra. Maintaining dignity in the face of condescension and discrimination takes special grace and courage.

Conclusion

The cultural soils into which we are born contain debilitating toxins and enriching nutrients. Cultivating the nutrients and neutralizing toxins begins early and continues throughout the lifespan. Among the early shifts in the margins of my own struggle are the following:

- Survival and constraints *toward* expanded vision and opportunity

- Isolation and loneliness *toward* family solidarity and community

- Inferiority and insecurity *toward* desired acceptance and confidence

- Faith rooted in fear and demands *toward* faith formed in trust and grace

- Power as exploitation and domination *toward* power as resilience and dignity

CHAPTER TWO

Early Movements from Poverty to Privilege

Expanding Horizons

As life on McKinley Road unfolded, my inner struggles intensified. We slowly began to emerge from adverse poverty. It was here my youngest brother, Joe, was born, thirteen years my junior. We began to fix up the house by covering the shingles with wood siding. Dad brought box lids from the mill to serve as sheetrock for indoor walls and ceilings. While in high school, indoor plumbing was installed, and with a pick and a shovel, we dug out three small rooms underneath the house, one of which housed a furnace. For the first time, I had a room to myself. It was damp, with water seeping through the porous cinderblock walls and standing underneath my bed. Though I was still embarrassed by the house compared to my peers' homes, it was more comfortable.

By age ten, I was earning money delivering the *Johnson City Press Chronicle* to about sixty customers. I delivered them after school either on my bicycle or a Texas cattle horse that Granddaddy chose for me at the local stock market. I paid twenty-four dollars for Sally! She was my pride and joy and even had a brand on her right front flank. I earned a lot of money for a kid who received no allowance—about eight dollars each week—from my paper route, and I occasionally did odd jobs for neighbors.

I quit one neighbor after weeding his garden all day in the hot sun. With a smirk, he gave me a dollar for the day's work. I wanted to use my dad's go-to cuss word, but instead, I looked at him and said, "I won't be back no more!" I guess I was more comfortable with my granddaddy's response to condescending charity.

Early on, I had modeled for me alternative ways of dealing with conflicts, perceived and real injustices, and power differentials. I continue to live with the tension between direct confrontation and a more nuanced response. Being a middle child, I developed a propensity for mediation more than confrontation, especially with my siblings, cousins, and peers. Like my mother and grandfather, I have been averse to conflict, but like my dad and granddad, I have been willing to resist bullying, defend those in need, and stay in the fight to the end.

School, sports, and work became avenues of expanded horizons, increased hope, and internal and external tension. I did well in school and developed a love for reading. My teachers at Midway encouraged me by giving me responsibilities. For example, I was selected as a "patrol officer." I arrived at school early, put on a special vest, was given a flag, and placed beside the road to slow traffic. It gave me a sense of importance and authority. I felt like somebody!

Midway School included students in grades one through eight. Typically, after completing eighth grade, students went to Jonesborough High School. That's where Edna and Jim attended until they dropped out after only a few months in the ninth grade. Mr. Howard, the principal and eighth-grade teacher, suggested I enroll in Training School. East Tennessee State College (now University) was founded as a "teachers' college," and Training School was part of the university. I'm not sure why this appealed to me, but I applied and interviewed with the director of the Training School, Dr. Ralph Clark.

Dad accompanied me to Dr. Clark's office. I felt insecure, though excited. Going to Training School would set me apart from my Midway classmates and the kids on McKinley Road. Dad and I were both intimidated by Dr. Clark's education and "fancy" talk. We spoke as little as possible. I was delighted when he said I would be admitted! In addition to being an immediate boost to my self-confidence, the decision was one of the most formative of my life.

Although the campus was only three miles from home, it represented a totally different world. Training School students were predominantly from educated, middle- and upper-class, professional families. My peers assumed they would go to college and be lawyers, doctors, engineers, teachers, or business owners. Only one member of our extended family had a college education. My peers used proper grammar, pronounced words differently, went on vacations, attended movies, dressed in stylish clothing, and traveled out of East Tennessee. They drove late-model cars, while Dad dropped me off in an old Chevrolet with faded paint and dented fender. After school, I either walked or hitchhiked the mile to the textile mill, where I waited for Dad's shift to end for the trip back to the real world of McKinley Road.

The tension between the two worlds intensified. I became increasingly uneasy with my native world. I kept the two worlds separate, never letting school friends know where I lived. I was ashamed of my house and embarrassed that my parents weren't educated and "cultured" like my classmates' parents. There were occasional painful reminders that poverty was more than the absence of money.

One such incident reminded me that how I talked wasn't right. After a class session, I asked the teacher about a math problem. As I pointed to the problem, I asked, "Can you help me with that problem *thar*?" The teacher, in silence, wrote, "T-H-E-R-E," and asked, "How do you pronounce that word?" I responded, "THAR!" "Do you see an A-R in that word?" Blushing with embarrassment, I barely whispered, "No, sir." "Kenneth, you need to learn to speak correctly." I left humiliated. That's the way everyone I loved talked!

Other similar incidents occurred. While in the shower after baseball practice, a teammate flipped me with a towel. I chased him, declaring, "I'm going to whoop the 'far' out of you!" He stopped in his tracks and bent over in laughter. "You are going to do what?" I repeated what I had said, and the room erupted in laughter. "I guess you mean you are going to whip me." Being flipped by the towel didn't hurt nearly as much as being laughed at for not "speaking correctly."

Training School teachers and classmates contributed overall to a more positive self-image. I joined the newspaper staff, was admitted to the Beta Club, and was elected class president in the tenth and twelfth grades. Classmates voted me "Best All Around" in our senior year. But the contrast between my two worlds continued, and an "imposter syndrome" developed early. I assumed they would not be as affirming if they knew where I lived and how inferior I felt. I was too insecure to date. I couldn't pick a girl up in my dad's old Chevrolet, plus I lacked social graces. I had never been to a movie theater. What would we do on a date? The person they knew at Training School was an imposter!

Full immersion in the Protestant work ethic put me on the road from poverty to privilege. The entrenched values of diligence, perseverance, and determination were paying off. I was living in two worlds: the world of the working poor and the emerging world of the middle class and upwardly mobile. On the surface, life was good. However, feelings of inferiority and insecurity persisted. In which world do I belong? In the world of Training School, I felt like a pretender. In the world of McKinley Road, I was becoming a restless stranger. Who am I, really? Where do

I really belong—among the marginalized or among the privileged? Can I live in both worlds with peace?

God as the Good Shepherd

For some reason, we dropped out of church after moving to McKinley Road, except for occasional attendance at citywide crusades and camp meetings. But when I was eleven, Mom and Dad announced we were returning to the Baptist church. I objected and asked if I could attend the Methodist Church just down the road. They agreed to my compromise. It was one of those pivotal decisions that would set the course of my life to this day.

I remember my first Sunday at McKinley Methodist Church. After doing the morning chores and delivering the Sunday papers, I walked to the church. It was a small, white-frame, picturesque building located in a sharp curve in the road. The railroad was on one side of the road, and across the tracks was Granddaddy's and Grandma's house. Near the church was a cemetery with granite tombstones, two outhouses—one for women, one for men—and a few trees.

I walked hesitantly into the small vestibule, where Mr. Peters greeted me and pointed me to the classroom for elementary kids. As I approached the doorway, Mrs. Mahoney spotted me. She announced with glee, "We have a visitor this morning, boys and girls!" I slowly, shyly, entered the room. Mrs. Mahoney then did something I had never experienced in church. SHE HUGGED ME! The only person I recall hugging me in church was my mother, who often put her arm around me while I slept during the sermon. Mrs. Mahoney's hug produced a far different feeling than I had when attending the crusades, camp meetings, and Baptist church. The lesson that morning was also different.

Although more than seventy years ago, I still remember the Bible story and the picture on the small table. The lesson was about the Good Shepherd and lost sheep. The teaching picture portrayed a shepherd retrieving a little lamb lodged on a branch protruding from the rocks over a cleft. Mrs. Mahoney explained that a little lamb had wandered away from the flock and was lost. The shepherd searched all night for the lost member of the flock. Upon rescuing it, the shepherd placed the frightened sheep on his shoulders and carried it back to the fold.

Her next statement was life-changing. Mrs. Mahoney said, "God is like that shepherd. God loves every one of us and is always looking for us when we are lost. Even though there are ninety-nine other sheep, God is willing to risk losing them to find one lamb that is lost."

It had never occurred to me that God was like a "Good Shepherd." God was more the landlord who held me over the rain barrel. God was like the shouting preachers who warned that God was going to bring the world to a catastrophic end, activate the rapture, and leave lost sheep behind "to weep and wail and gnash their teeth." I had not made the connection that God was more like my parents or my beloved grandfather than a stern judge, angry preacher, or hateful landlord!

Therein began my conversion, my journey toward trusting God rather than being terrorized by God. There began a lifelong struggle to love God rather than fear God, trust God rather than be intimidated by God, and serve God out of gratitude for being found rather than panic at being eternally lost. That Sunday morning seven decades ago marked the beginning of a life lived in church, for the church, and with the church. That morning, I found an extended family beyond my blood kin. I was initiated into that family first with a hug from Mrs. Mahoney. I have often wondered if it would have been different had she not hugged me. On that morning, Mrs. Mahoney was the Good Shepherd who found a lost, shy sharecropper's boy who bore the scars of poverty and marginalization and gently brought him into a new way of knowing God and what it means to be a child of God. I never missed a Sunday in Sunday School after that. Looking back, I now see that she spurred my theological imagination and sowed the seeds of a pastoral practice on the margins.

I was at the church almost every time the doors opened, including the revivals. But I wasn't sure "I had been saved." That was the language familiar to my parents and grandparents, and in that heavily Baptist and Pentecostal community, it was the prevailing religious ethos. I wanted "to be saved," but I wasn't sure how I was supposed to feel or what to do. During a revival meeting in the summer of 1952, I felt it was time to do something. One Sunday night, I wondered if I should go to the altar during the invitation. I thought about it when I went home and all the next day. I was embarrassed to say anything to my parents or anyone. All my family members were still attending the Baptist church and were not part of my experience at McKinley Methodist.

On Monday night of the revival, the preacher gave the invitation and announced that we would be singing "I Surrender All." A church member came to where I sat on the back row with some neighborhood boys. She put her arm around me and said, "Kenneth, don't you think it is time for you to go to the altar and accept Jesus as your Lord and Savior?" I am not sure of all the psychological dynamics and social pressure involved, but I walked to the altar, knelt, and asked Jesus to forgive me and "save me." A couple of others joined me, and several adults surrounded us, including Mrs. Mahoney. Following the closing prayer, members of the congregation came and hugged us.

I went home after the service and told my mother what had happened. She seemed delighted and said, "I'm proud of you." Although I do not consider that experience "my conversion," it was a part of the grace that continues to "convert" me. While I long ago moved away from that religious ethos and means of initiation into the Christian church, I realize that the theological perspectives and pastoral practices that have characterized my life and ministry were forged in this dominant southern ethos and rural Appalachia culture in the 1940s and 1950s.

Conflicting images of God as stern judge versus gentle shepherd, religion as harsh judgment with apocalyptic consequences versus religion as a source of redemption, feelings of inferiority and cultural deprivation versus assurance of acceptance and forgiveness as a beloved child of God—these and other dichotomies reflect conflicts within the broader Appalachian culture with its inequities of power and wealth and the harsh realities of being part of the underclass in a region exploited for its rich natural resources and cheap labor.

Reverend Myers suggested the next step in following Jesus was to be baptized and received into the church membership. He told me I could receive baptism by immersion, sprinkling, or pouring. Since my parents and siblings and most of my extended family members were either Baptist or Pentecostal and believed only in immersion, I chose to be immersed. McKinley Methodist had no facilities for such a mode of baptism, so Reverend Myers arranged for it to take place in the swimming pool of Munsey Memorial Methodist Church in Johnson City.

On a Sunday afternoon in 1952, we gathered at the swimming pool with a small group from the McKinley congregation and my parents. I was given no instruction on what baptism meant, only that it was a requirement for church membership. It was an unremarkable experience, the meaning of which was to be understood decades later. Little did I realize then that I was being baptized into Jesus Christ and that baptism would be the source and sign of my identity and purpose in life.

My involvement in McKinley Church deepened as I attended Sunday School, worship, and Methodist Youth Fellowship (MYF). In that small youth group, I was formed for future leadership and experienced what it meant to be part of a "connectional church." In the 1950s, youth included ages twelve through college, so I remained in a youth group until my junior year in college. It was as a youth that I spoke before the congregation for the first time. Since McKinley was part of a circuit, we regularly joined the youth from other small churches on the circuit for activities. The Methodist genius for connectional structure also involved us in sub-district, district, and conference events and activities. My church world grew through these events and relationships, and my involvement intensified.

I was invited to perform several roles as a youth, including serving as president of the MYF for four years, making announcements in the worship service, assisting Mrs. Mahoney in teaching children in Bible school, and even serving as church treasurer as a freshman in college. As a junior in high school, the church hired me as a custodian for sixteen dollars a month—my first paying job in a church. The duties included opening and closing the doors for Sunday morning and evening services and Wednesday night prayer meetings; firing the furnace in the winter, requiring I get up at 4:30 every Sunday morning; cleaning the church; arranging chairs; and mowing the lawn, including the cemetery. Trimming around tombstones was back-breaking, and mowing with a reel-type push mower required time and energy. Being the janitor taught me a lot about church!

Succeeding Reverend Myers as pastor was John Bacon, a recent graduate of Candler School of Theology. He was young, athletic, and vitally engaged with youth. He frequently invited the guys to join him in "touch football" or "catch" baseball and pickup basketball games. He encouraged me to participate in district and conference events, and through his influence, I began to think about becoming a Methodist pastor.

John Bacon helped me attend the National Youth Convocation held at Purdue University, where youth from across the country gathered. I, along with other youth from Holston Conference, rode buses to the event. Since I had rarely traveled outside the region, I was insecure and hesitant. Still, I joined the group. There, we interacted with diverse youth and adults and heard speakers from around the world. It was there that I heard my first Black American preacher, a tall, young, stately man introduced as "Doctor." It was James S. Thomas. I never thought I would meet him personally, much less be a friend and colleague in the Council of Bishops years later!

Involvement in church activities exposed me to alternative expressions of religion and faith. I became involved in an ecumenical youth organization in Johnson City, an outgrowth of the citywide ministerial association, which sponsored an annual Appalachian Preaching Mission.[1] The preachers were the antithesis of the "hellfire and damnation" preachers of my early childhood, and they helped reform my image of the church and my

---

[1] The preachers were from mainline denominations and included such luminaries as Carlyle Marney, Ernest Campbell, James Cleland, and Louis Evans.

understanding of the Christian faith. While representing different denominations, they communicated a spirit of oneness and forged a vision of the church as a community of compassion and grace rather than a place of fear, judgment, and everlasting damnation. The preachers also represented an alternative image from the screaming preachers of earlier childhood.

Experientially, I was moving away from the world of poverty with its privations and into a world of privilege and abundance of opportunity and resources. Yet, those worlds remained separate and segregated. I did not know if the two worlds could even be reconciled.

The Crucial Bridge Person Between My Two Worlds

Most pivotal experiences happen amid the routine and ordinary, and only in retrospect is their importance recognized. Such was my attendance at the Holston Conference Youth Assembly at Emory and Henry College in 1959.

A particular girl caught my attention during an evening of "folk games," a euphemism for dancing. While she was talking with a group of girls, I pointed her out to my roommate at the conference and asked if he knew her. "Oh, that's Linda Miller. She's my classmate here at Emory and Henry. I'll introduce you." And he did. I learned she was from Elizabethton and a sophomore majoring in religious education. The brief conversation was our only encounter during the week, but I was always conscious of her presence.

Weeks later, someone in youth group suggested we invite a student to speak to us about attending a church-related college. I immediately thought of the young woman I had met at Emory and Henry and volunteered to ask her to speak to our group. I called Linda, introduced myself, and explained that we had met at the youth assembly. She didn't remember me.

A rising junior at Emory and Henry, Linda gladly accepted the invitation, and my life hasn't been the same since! I'm not sure I heard anything she said that evening in 1959.[2] I was too preoccupied with asking her out. How would I ask her? I thought she probably had a boyfriend, and I knew I couldn't compete with her college classmates. I was too insecure to ask her out that evening. Only later did I muster enough courage to call her and ask if she wanted to attend a baseball game. To my surprise and sheer delight, she said, "Yes."

I fretted over what to wear and what Linda would think about the old car I would drive. My dad had traded the old beat-up 1947 Chevrolet for a blue 1950 Chevy. At least it had no dents. I washed and shined it and cleaned the interior. I drove nervously to her home in Elizabethton, about ten miles away. She lived in a relatively new house on a recently developed street that had become *the* place to live in Elizabethton. By today's standards, it is a very modest house, but it was a castle compared to where I lived.

---

[2] Upon Linda's death more than sixty years after that Sunday evening, I found a handwritten copy of the speech she gave that night.

I learned quickly that her parents knew my parents, that my grandmother had taught Linda's mother in Sunday School, and that both parents worked at the North American Rayon plant in Elizabethton. I immediately felt relieved and very much accepted by them. My defenses dropped with the awareness that Linda's heritage included some similarities with mine, though my socio-economic experience was more compatible with that of her parents' childhood.

Linda's parents, Mack and Leila, had already moved into the middle class. They had only one child and earned dual incomes. Leila had graduated from Jonesborough High School and had a well-paying job. They valued hard work as the way out of poverty and emphasized education as a means to higher status and better jobs. Mack had dropped out of school at fourteen to provide income for the family. Some thirty years later, he earned his GED by correspondence. In addition to his "swing shift" work at the rayon plant, he did landscaping to add to the family income. The Millers had bought a little one-room cabin on Watauga Lake and spent time there in the summers.

Linda and I saw one another several times during the summer of 1959, mostly in district youth activities, attending church, and visits to her home and the lake. We were both officers in the district MYF, which provided occasions to be together and to work on projects and events. I dreaded Linda's return to Emory and Henry because it was more than an hour's drive away. We promised to write, and she returned home several weekends.

I finally got up enough courage to invite Linda to visit my family in our home, but I did so with much fear and trembling. I was embarrassed for her to see the house and nervous for her to meet my parents, especially Dad. Dad paid no attention to etiquette and appropriate attire. He was uninhibited about belching, going barefoot, or clipping his toenails. He was often angry and never attempted to impress anyone, especially those considered "above him."

On a Sunday afternoon, we drove up to the house that now had white siding. We arrived to find Mom and Dad in the small living room. Dad was seated in his usual chair, unshaven, barefoot, wearing work pants and a white, sleeveless undershirt. He didn't get up as I introduced Linda. Mom was quiet and shy. Dad's initial conversation was limited to "hello." Linda graciously and warmly greeted them. The conversation thankfully picked up when we talked about Linda's parents and their work at the Elizabethton plant. Mom remembered Leila from their childhood days at McKinley and confided to me later that she had felt uncomfortable in her presence. But the visit was pleasant and brief. Years later, Linda admitted she was "shocked" to learn of the conditions I lived in, though it did not diminish her care for me.

Linda, in many ways, became a "bridge person." Whereas I had lived in divided worlds with others outside McKinley Road, she was the first to know my McKinley Road world *and* the middle-class world of Training School, college, and the broader church. She didn't reject my native world, make fun of it, or put me down. To do so would have been to reject part of her parents' upbringing and her own heritage. Maybe it was the blindness of romance, but she expressed no hesitancy to continue our relationship after the visit.

Linda began bridging another world and became a means of integrating religion, education, and economics. She told me about religion courses at Emory and Henry. As a Christian education major, she took Bible, ethics, and theology courses. One professor was particularly important to her—Dr. Robert Mielke. She had a course in the prophets with Dr. Mielke, and our first argument resulted from a discussion of Isaiah. The question was whether Isaiah predicted the coming of Jesus in Isaiah 7:14 with the promise of "a virgin shall conceive and bear a son" or if the reference was to a child born in Isaiah's time. I had no doubt! In my opinion, it was self-evident, and the Bible didn't make mistakes. Well, Linda shared the alternative, that "virgin" can be translated as "young woman," and the promise had to be interpreted in historical and literary context. That was another step out of fundamentalism for me! While I had read about interpreting the Bible in context, the argument with Linda forced me to take it seriously.

I was drawn to ordained ministry as a vocation largely through the quiet influence of John Bacon and the image of pastors I had witnessed through conference activities and the Appalachian Preaching mission. Now Linda's commitment to Christian education added to the lure of the church as the context for my vocation. With John Bacon's help and Linda's encouragement, I was licensed as a local pastor at nineteen! Another step, moving from poverty to privilege, from the homogeneous world of McKinley Road toward an ever-expanding horizon only imagined in my walks across the hills of eastern Tennessee.

"Just Go Out There and Love Them"

In May 1960, I received a surprising call from the district superintendent, Dr. Frank Porter, inviting me to serve as the student pastor of Watauga Methodist Church. Watauga was a small community with a population of less than four hundred located along the banks of the Watauga River and about three miles northeast of Johnson City. The only industry in the community was a large rock quarry. There was a country store, post office, and "mill" which ground corn and supplied local farmers. The largest landowner was the St. John family, who owned the mill and surrounding farmland. The church had a membership of fifty-six and an average attendance of twenty-two. The small, white-frame church was tucked on a hillside above the river and railroad tracks.

Once given the appointment, I suddenly realized I had no idea what to do next! I asked Dr. Porter, "Do you have any instructions for me?" He answered, "Just go out there and love the people."

The first step was to visit the church and community. I drove up the narrow dirt road, crossed the railroad tracks, and parked on the church lawn. I entered the church with excitement and anticipation. Inside was the sanctuary, a small storage room, two restrooms, and a table with small chairs that served as the "children's classroom."

As I walked the grounds and stood looking across the surrounding hillsides, Mr. Feathers approached. He lived in a large white house overlooking the church grounds. "Are you our new preacher?" he asked. "We are glad to have you. We really like to have young student pastors. In fact, we consider giving young pastors a start to be part of our purpose."

Before my first Sunday, I had visited all the active members. I patterned the first worship service after the services of my home church. There was no printed bulletin, and the approach was informal, with no robes or choir.

Kate ("Aunt Kate" as she was called) played the piano. She was the congregation's "character." A large woman in her late fifties, she always spoke in high volume. Her tanned complexion, robust arms and shoulders were evidence of her hard work in the hot sun. Kate walked down the railroad for each service, including night services. She was fearless, uninhibited, and boisterous! She hit the piano keys as though chopping weeds in the cornfield—hard, firm strokes. On my first Sunday, I announced the opening hymn as number six, "Holy, Holy, Holy." We made it through the first and second verses with ease. Then, a breeze through the nearby window turned the page of Aunt Kate's book, and she didn't notice the change. She suddenly started playing the accompaniment to hymn number seven, "O Worship the King." We stopped, confused. Aunt Kate blurted out, "Oops! Wrong page!" Members of the congregation smiled as though nothing unusual had happened.

Aunt Kate's brother, Mitch, died during my first year as pastor. Kate asked me to assist Dr. William Rigel in the funeral service. Dr. Rigel was the pastor emeritus of Central Baptist Church in Johnson City and a former professor of mine at East Tennessee State University (ETSU). As we waited for the service to begin, he asked, "Is this your first funeral, son?" I answered, "Yes," and he explained this was his 990th funeral. "I suppose you get used to it after a while, don't you?" I responded. He answered immediately, "Oh, no, you never get used to it. If you ever do, don't have any more funerals."

My experience as a student pastor was enhanced by classes at ETSU. I was excited when Dr. Mielke, Linda's favorite professor at Emory and Henry, joined the ETSU faculty. The classes with him enabled me to reflect intellectually on ministry and helped me think critically about my own faith. Along with courses in literature, creative writing, and sociology, I began to integrate my religious perspectives with philosophical and theological reflection. My diverse worlds on McKinley Road, ETSU, and now Watauga were slowly emerging as one world through the church. Learning to read the Bible in its historical, literary, and theological context was stimulating and instructive. While I was naïve and my knowledge was superficial, I felt at home in the world of ideas, critical reflection, and learning.

Preaching every Sunday morning and leading studies on Sunday evenings were exciting adventures. I was eager to share my new insights with the congregation, often to their dismay. For example, I announced we would study "other religions" on Sunday evenings. Following the first session on Islam, Sarah protested, "Kenneth, I won't be coming back on Sunday nights. I thought we were going to talk about the Baptists, Presbyterians, and Church of God. I never heard of Muslims, and I don't see any reason to know about them." What a different world!

Linda was very much accepted and appreciated by the Watauga congregation. She attended services when home from college. The summer between her junior and senior years, we talked about getting married. I didn't want to be separated from her and dreaded when she left for her final year in college. Eleven months older than me, she was a year ahead of me in school.

We got engaged and set the date for the following summer, June 30, 1961. Although I would only be twenty, I was still the oldest of my siblings to marry. Edna had married at fifteen, Jim at seventeen, and Dennis at sixteen.

During the fall semester, Linda shared that a person from Wesley Theological Seminary in Washington, D.C., would be visiting the campus to talk with prospective students. John Baxter Howes was the director of admissions and field placement. He told us about the new seminary, now located on the campus of the American University, and indicated that a scholarship would likely be available and that he would work toward securing a student pastoral appointment.

The prospects of living in Washington were exciting! We indicated it would be another year, 1962, before I would graduate but that we were interested. Now the plan to attend seminary was firmly implanted, and the pull to Washington became stronger as I continued as a college student and part-time pastor for another eighteen months.

Linda graduated in May 1961 with a degree in Christian education, and we married the next month at First Methodist Church in Elizabethton. It was a happy occasion attended by a mixture of people. My parents were uncomfortable, though. It was their first time attending a formal wedding, with a rehearsal dinner and reception. I felt for them, but everyone treated them with respect and dignity.

My annual salary was twelve hundred dollars, and we had no parsonage. The St. Johns invited us to live on their farm in the three-room house previously used as servants' quarters. Church members furnished the house with unused items. Linda got a job as a secretary in the Department of Health at ETSU, enabling us to drive to school/work together each day. It was a transition year as I completed college, and Linda and I forged a bond of love that would grow over the next half-century.

In August, my beloved Granddaddy Walker died

unexpectedly from a stroke at age sixty-seven. His death devastated us. He had been a steady, wise, caring, and consistent presence in our lives. My dad cried in front of us for the first time as he affirmed that Granddaddy had been his father, too. The whole community was in mourning. Granddaddy had plowed their gardens, worked their fields, given them vegetables, befriended their children, and aided them in times of distress.

Granddaddy's funeral drew an overflow crowd at McKinley Church. Unlike Granny, shouting and outward demonstrative religion made him uncomfortable, so he did not attend church often. He never held an office or taught a class as Granny had done. He was embarrassed when, on occasion, she asked him to say grace at meals. His primary faith practices were gentleness, honesty, compassion, hard work, and simple gestures of kindness—especially toward kids and those he called "little people" (like himself). I never heard him say an unkind word about anyone, and his response to a negative judgment of another was often, "Now, we don't know the whole story."

May 1962 marked a major transition with graduation and an appointment as a student pastor in the Baltimore-Washington Conference. We left the "pawpaw patch" of our birth, leaving behind our kin and the rich cultural roots that had nurtured us into adulthood. Dramatic shifts in our relationships, thinking, and experience awaited. Comfortable boundaries of thinking and relating were about to be forever changed.

Conclusion

Methodists talk a lot about "prevenient grace," the grace that precedes our awareness of it. Perhaps it's another name for the foundational relationships and experiences that prod, pull, and woo us toward wholeness and oneness. Only in retrospect do we usually recognize grace's presence. Our lives unfold within an ineffable mystery filled with inexplicable longings, connections, and events.

The odyssey from the margins to the mainstream is filled with paradoxes. The poverty and culture from which I sought to flee contained the gifts for which I longed. From wrestling with those paradoxes came deeper insights, broadened circles of community, and an ever-expanding vision of life's meaning and purpose. The rich nutrients and underpinning roots of the Appalachian "pawpaw patch" provided the foundation for the continued shifting of the margins of my participation in an ever-expanding world.

The worlds of poverty and privilege collided early as the grip of poverty's constraints slackened, and new possibilities appeared on the horizon. Exposure to worlds beyond the familiar awakened tensions and conflicts within me and in relationships. Those tensions and conflicts stretched the margins *from* …

- Fatalistic acceptance of things as they were *toward* greater expectations for change
- Passive acquiescence to injustice and oppression *toward* courage to resist

- Assumed powerlessness *toward* presumed personal agency

- Reflective withdrawal *toward* initiative in entering new relationships

- Church as a place of fear/oppression *toward* church as a redemptive bridge/community

- Salvation as escape from eternal damnation *toward* salvation as personal and social integration

- God as a stern judge who terrorizes *toward* God as retrieving shepherd and nurturing parent

- Faith as dogmatic certainty *toward* faith as grace and mystery

CHAPTER THREE

A Whole New World and a Radical Shift

Seminary in Washington, D.C.

Leaving the small, rural Watauga community and the hills of eastern Tennessee for Wesley Seminary in the bustling Washington, D.C., urban area was a thrilling and scary adventure. The excitement, however, overshadowed the fear. With our meager belongings packed in a small U-Haul trailer latched behind our 1956 Chevrolet, we headed up Highway 11E through the Shenandoah Valley of Virginia. It was June 1962, and Interstate 81 had not been completed, so the trip took approximately twelve hours.

Dr. Howes at Wesley helped arrange a student pastoral appointment for me to a two-point charge, Hunting Hill and MacDonald Chapel, located in Montgomery County, Maryland, about thirty minutes from the seminary campus. The two congregations provided an apartment in Gaithersburg for their shared pastor. It was considerably upscale from the house we had left, and Gaithersburg was rapidly transitioning from a rural, small town to a thriving suburb of the nation's capital. The movement from poverty to privilege accelerated.

Both the pastoral assignment and Wesley Seminary would be intense ventures in learning and growing over the next three years. These were the turbulent 1960s with the Vietnam War, the civil rights struggle, the rise of "black power" in the streets and on campuses, the Cuban missile crisis and acknowledged threat of nuclear annihilation, the aftermath of Joseph McCarthy's hunt for communists within existing American institutions, the John Birch Society's impact on local communities, the political polarization based largely on race with the hate-filled rhetoric of George Wallace, Ross Barnett, Lester Maddox, Bull Connors, and others.

Indeed, those were "the best of times and the worst of times." Conventional moral and ethical standards were being questioned as the "sexual revolution," emerging drug culture, rock-and-roll music, and suspicion of traditional forms of authority threatened stability based on certainty and shared values. An expression heard often was, "Everything we thought was nailed down is coming loose." It was a time of pushing boundaries and exploring new ways of thinking and behaving. What a time to be engaged in theological education in the nation's capital!

I entered seminary with high expectations and was never disappointed. When I arrived on campus for the fall 1962 semester, the buildings were new, and the excitement of faculty and staff was evident. Wesley Seminary was the culmination of dreams and planning by three formidable

Methodist leaders: Bishop G. Bromley Oxnam, bishop of the Baltimore/Washington Conference; Norman L. Trott, president of the seminary; and Hurst Anderson, the president of American University. Oxnam received national notoriety from his appearance before the House Committee on Un-American Activities chaired by Senator Joseph McCarthy. Oxnam's progressive social views attracted the committee's attention, and he was labeled as a communist sympathizer. His vigorous public defense on July 21, 1953, did much to expose the irresponsibility of the committee. The seminary chapel bears his name, signifying his impact on the seminary's vision and mission.

The front of the chapel faces Massachusetts Avenue, which carries heavy traffic to and from the centers of governmental power and world influence. Anchored on the outside wall is a figure of Christ with uplifted, outstretched hands. Our professors made sure the turbulent events of the 1960s were seen as arenas of God's action and the church's mission.

Orientation week included sharing of the seminary's history and its move from rural Maryland to Washington, with the layout and architecture of the campus serving as sermons in stone. The message was indelibly etched in my mind: Here, you are expected to learn and experience God and the Christian faith as expressed in the Wesleyan tradition, be formed as pastors who engage the complex world, and devote yourself to knowledge and vital piety. I was being oriented toward a whole new world. It was a different planet from McKinley Road, and Oxnam Chapel felt like a cathedral compared to McKinley and Watauga Methodist Churches.

At the opening service during orientation, I was immediately exposed to a style of worship that my grandmother would have rebelled against as "Catholic." The liturgy was formal, printed on a bulletin, with responses I did not know. The preacher, Dr. Trott, used a manuscript and wore a robe. A pipe organ accompanied the music, and the hymns were largely unfamiliar.

Imposter Syndrome

Orientation week also included taking a series of intellectual and psychological tests. Dr. Earl Ferguson, professor of Preaching and Pastoral Theology, had championed psychological tests for entering students. He often quoted Carl Patton: "The making of a preacher is the making of a person." The tension between the worlds of McKinley Road and Wesley Seminary surfaced during the testing process. I feared my insecurities and phoniness would be exposed, and the tests would reveal to the faculty that I was only a dumb hillbilly masquerading as a seminary student.

I met with Dr. Ferguson to discuss the results. I was in awe of him. He had preached a brilliant sermon in chapel. He was known as a tough professor, with his classes labeled "Fergutory." He was formal, always dressed in a suit, white shirt, and tie. He graduated from DePauw University with

Phi Beta Kappa honors and received his Ph.D. from Boston University School of Theology. He served as minister of the Harvard Epworth Church, director of Harvard's Wesley Foundation, and lecturer in homiletics at Boston School of Theology. He was everything I wasn't—well-educated, intelligent, articulate, self-assured, and prominent. Now I sat in his office, insecure, shy, and about to be exposed as a phony unqualified to be on campus.

Dr. Ferguson sensed my unease and discomfort. He began, "We are glad you have chosen to come to Wesley, and we look forward to working with you for the next three years." He then identified issues that surfaced in the testing. One was the conflict between my low scores on the standardized measures of intellectual and academic ability and my high grades in college. I was embarrassed to have my stupidity confirmed! But the subsequent conversation began healing the inner conflict I had felt all my life. He asked about my background, and for the first time, I shared about my world of McKinley Road, the son of Appalachian sharecropper/millworker parents. He asked if I read books in the home as a child, and I replied that the only book we had was the Bible. With a rare smile, he responded, "Well, if you only have one, that's the right choice."

Dr. Ferguson remarked that he was initially concerned and wondered if I could do the required academic work. I admitted I didn't feel smart but that I would work hard. He then said, "Kenneth, I suspect your grades are more indicative of your ability than the standardized test scores." He added that standardized tests have a class bias, presume a certain vocabulary level, and do not measure motivation, which is at least as important as native intellect.

The session continued with Dr. Ferguson drawing the relationship between the psychological and academic tests. The psychological tests revealed intense feelings of inferiority coupled with perfectionism and a tendency toward depression. Dr. Ferguson stated that my feelings of inferiority were more evident in the standardized mental tests than in my academic ability. He speculated that I feel less threatened and more confident when I am tested for subject content. However, when I feel I am being tested for "intelligence" or "personality," my inferiority feelings take over, and I see myself as incapable and threatened. The session with Dr. Ferguson was one of the most far-reaching conversations of my life.

Transformative Learning and "Fergutory"

We were fortunate to live within a thirty-minute drive of the campus. Classes were held Tuesday through Friday, and I drove from Gaithersburg each morning. Linda got a job as the secretary at St. Dunstan's Episcopal Church, a mile from the seminary. She only worked two days each week, enabling her to audit a few courses. Seminary was, therefore, a joint venture, and her background in Christian education equipped her to be a valued conversation partner in my theological education.

The diversity of the student body was a stark contrast to my previous experience. The presence of non-White persons was a major difference. Since women had not been widely received into ordained ministry, the few in class were studying to become Christian education directors. Students were predominantly from the northeastern U.S.—Maryland, Pennsylvania, Delaware, New York, and New Jersey, with Virginia having a large number. I was the only student from Tennessee. My accent was an obvious exception and a cause for laughter by many—and an embarrassment for me. My speech pattern was confronted early in the classroom.

I had taken speech in college, but it was taught by a native East Tennessean who raised no concerns about *how* I spoke beyond using correct grammar. At Wesley, however, my Tennessee accent with the flat "i" and omitted consonants—preachin', teachin', singin', prayin', talkin'—was considered an impediment in need of correction. A remedial speech course was required. I had never formed the ending "g" sound and had great difficulty learning to do so. Professor Moyer sought to make every preacher speak as crisply as Walter Cronkite. I worked hard to change my way of speaking—even practicing into a tape recorder—and to lose my "hillbilly accent."

Though I was pleased that I learned to "talk correctly" in cosmopolitan society, the process added to the tension between my poverty culture and the world of privilege and success. My family now thought I "talked fancy" and seemed suspicious that I might be negatively judging their speech, though I never dared correct their grammar or suggest they weren't "speaking correctly." I did not want them to experience the embarrassment I had experienced for being corrected!

I was particularly impressed with the presence of Black Americans. East Tennessee had very few Black Americans, and I went to segregated schools all the way through college. As racial tensions increased and students became active in civil rights efforts, I encountered firsthand the pain inflicted on Blacks. One Black American classmate, a muscular, former college football player and student pastor on the eastern shore of Maryland, particularly fascinated me. He came to class one morning with bruises on his face. He had participated in a demonstration, was beaten by police, and spent the weekend in jail. He was a gentle, gracious man, a model of Christian witness and courage. He and others personalized the racism and injustice now increasingly visible across the country. I was breaking out of the provincialism of my segregated roots.

Old Testament, taught by Dr. Lowell B. Hazzard, was my favorite first-semester course. Dr. Hazzard was a brilliant lecturer who quoted long passages from memory. One of his greatest gifts was relating scripture to contemporary issues. Study of the eighth-century prophets included a discussion of the Cuban missile crisis and the move toward the Vietnam War. Study of the prophets precipitated reflections on current policy discussions in Congress related to poverty, taxation, and agriculture. I began to see that the poverty that had so shaped my thinking had deep theological implications. Amos and Micah, products of rural culture, gave voice to my repressed anger at the sharecropping and millworker systems that exploited the poor. Dr. Hazzard helped me see with fresh eyes that God cares for the vulnerable, the orphans, the widows, and landless people—like my family.

Dr. Hazzard's commitment to formation and information meant that he paid attention to students' actions outside the classroom, and he never hesitated to confront us with unacceptable behavior. A student posted "JESUS SAVES" on the bulletin board outside Dr. Hazzard's office. Someone came along and wrote underneath the words "GREEN STAMPS." Green Stamps were used in those days like coupons today. Several students were reading the bulletin board before class, many laughing scornfully at the clever retort to "JESUS SAVES." Emerging from his office, Dr. Hazzard took down both signs and carried them into the classroom. He asked rhetorically, "What do you find funny about this?" He then affirmed that, indeed, Jesus Christ saves, and if we think that is a joke, we need to leave seminary. Next, he lifted the "GREEN STAMPS" as a metaphor for how we so easily wed the market with Jesus.

Why did this incident stick in my mind all these years? "JESUS SAVES" was part of the religious milieu of my boyhood and youth. It was painted on barns and billboards along the highways. It was the mantra of revivalist preachers and the underlying assumption of evangelical preaching. "Be saved" and "accept Jesus as your personal savior" prefaced invitations that concluded most worship services in those small local congregations, especially if they were Baptists. I had responded to such an invitation a decade earlier. The language was not "in vogue" in my current context, but it was part of my heritage and formation. Could it be that Dr. Hazzard's respect for the meaning of the phrase and refusal to put it aside encouraged me to make peace with my conservative, fundamentalist background and to integrate it into my experience of God in Christ?

I wasn't hostile toward the evangelicalism of my childhood; that would have meant hostility toward persons like my parents and grandparents, who embodied the best of evangelical culture. However, I longed for freedom from the fear, rigidity, legalism, and anti-intellectualism that continued to haunt me.

It was in systematic theology class that the news came on November 22, 1963, of the shooting of President Kennedy. Dr. Gilmore immediately offered prayer and then dismissed the session. When I arrived, Linda was staring at the television. Soon, Walter Cronkite struggled to announce President Kennedy's death. Suddenly, the world seemed to stop. A dark cloud of gloom and despair seemed to cover the earth. We were stunned with disbelief! We remained glued to the television, watching every detail as the search for the assassin took place and Oswald was finally apprehended. It was an intense time that shattered and dampened the optimism that had been so pervasive since we left Tennessee and entered the fast, exciting world of Washington, D.C.

Fortunately, the faculty helped us grapple with the

theological questions now confronting us: Had we put too much trust in government and the president? What is God's action on the world stage? Such times moved theological education from the abstract to the real. Making sense of suffering, injustice, political unrest, racial hatred, and violence in relation to God's mission was embedded within the curriculum and teaching of the seminary. There was no discontinuity between what was happening in the classrooms and the events on the streets of Washington and Dallas.

The most personally transformative class was Dr. Ferguson's "Sermonic Clinic," which focused on preparing, delivering, and critiquing sermons. Students had labeled this class "Fergutory," reflecting the professor's reputation for brutal analysis of sermons. Soon, I experienced "Fergutory."

When my time to preach came, I used the sermon I preached on Easter. After all, the congregations had been very affirming. The sermon had two basic points: the resurrection brings forgiveness, and the resurrection brings hope. Typically, following delivery, the preacher of the day remained in front of the class for feedback from the students and Dr. Ferguson. The students were short on both praise and criticism as I stood before them. Dr. Ferguson gave only criticism. With calm firmness, he asked, "What do you mean by resurrection? Is resurrection primarily about the resuscitation of a corpse?"

I frankly had never raised such questions, and, as I told him, I assumed, indeed, the resurrection was about Jesus coming back to life. Dr. Ferguson asked, "Well, then, tell us how Jesus coming back to life makes forgiveness possible, and how does that bring hope, other than the possibility that we might be brought back to life after we die?" He kept pushing, suggesting I get at the deeper truth by asking, "How did the rumor 'he is risen' change the disciples?" He then used my sermon as an example of the problem of abstraction in preaching and the "clothesline" approach to sermons.

Indeed, I had preached on forgiveness and hope without defining either, and I offered a meaningless solution for guilt and despair. Dr. Ferguson peppered me with questions: What is the resurrection? How does it make a difference in our guilt and despair? Did the crucifixion and resurrection make possible something that was impossible before, or did the crucifixion and resurrection of Jesus reveal what has been in the heart and action of God from the very beginning? These questions raised by Dr. Ferguson on that painful day in 1964 continue to push the margins of my thinking.

Dr. Ferguson's negative response was devastating! After class, I drove home discouraged and embarrassed. Linda greeted me with the question, "How did it go?" I burst into tears! My confidence was shattered. It was more than a failure in one school assignment. Preaching is so much a part of our identity as pastors. The old feelings of insecurity, inferiority, and stupidity resurfaced with poignancy. Do I really belong in seminary? Linda's reassurance and reminder that the congregations responded positively to the sermon had little credibility. Dr. Ferguson was the expert.

I returned to campus the next morning with little sleep, despondent, discouraged, and embarrassed. Walking to class, I heard, "Wait up, Kenneth." It was Dr. Ferguson. There followed one of those seminal encounters of my life and subsequent ministry.

"Yesterday's class hurt, didn't it?" said Dr. Ferguson. "You don't realize how much it hurt," I replied. As he extended his arm and placed his hand on my shoulder, Dr. Ferguson spoke more gently than in the classroom, "Oh, I think I know. But, Kenneth, I assume you are here because you feel you have been called to preach. You need to understand why I am here. I am here to help make you the best preacher you can be."

Then he moved closer, and, extending his arm around my shoulder in a light embrace, he said, "And, Kenneth, I believe in you." More than a homiletical lesson was being taught. As he held me, he held me accountable. The essence of Christian discipleship was demonstrated: being held with compassion and being held accountable to our identity as a child of God. Previously, I had only experienced being held to strict accountability by Dr. Ferguson. I had not felt warmth or compassion from him. Now I understood his strict demands and high expectations were part of a larger purpose rather than an attempt to humiliate or dominate. Tears welled up as I thanked him. After that, I signed up for as many of his classes as possible.

A class taught by Dr. Haskell Miller, "The Church and Its Community," significantly influenced my ministry.

He emphasized how pastors must be as skilled in understanding the demographics, history, and social forces in the context as they are familiar with biblical texts. One assignment required us to walk the streets of a ghetto in southeast Washington and ask people in the neighborhood what they knew about the church nearby. Dr. Miller insisted one does not know a congregation apart from its relationship with the surrounding community. A brief encounter in that assignment established a practice that continued throughout my ministry. I approached an elderly Black American man sitting on the stoop of a tenement house within view of a church. After a brief greeting, I pointed toward the church and asked:

> "What can you tell me about that church?"
> "Nothin'! I don't know nothin' about it," he said.
> "What do they do up there?" I inquired.
> "They don't do nothin' but have church and leave,"
>   was his response.

No members lived in the neighborhood, and all were White. They gathered each Sunday from other parts of the city and suburbs, sang their hymns, said their prayers, collected the offering, and then drove back to their own comfortable neighborhoods, never interacting with the people living around their church building. From henceforth, as a pastor or bishop, I walked the streets surrounding local churches and asked how the neighbors perceived the church. Sadly, many of the responses echoed the comment I first heard in southeast Washington more than a half-century earlier.

The seminary experience was rapidly ending as graduation approached in May 1965. Dad, Mom, and my brother Joe drove from Johnson City to attend graduation, as did Linda's parents, Mack and Leila. My parents seldom ventured beyond eastern Tennessee. Still uncomfortable in the company of the educated and unfamiliar with formal gatherings, they wanted to be present for the graduation of their only child to finish college and now seminary.

A luncheon preceded the graduation ceremony. Sensing my parents' discomfort, we sat near the back of the room. As the meal concluded, Dr. Howes came to our table and requested I come to the front for a presentation. I had no idea what was about to happen. Dr. Trott, the seminary president, called on Dr. Ferguson to present the "American Bible Society Award," given to the student who showed the most improvement in the public reading and interpretation of scripture. Although it may seem like a minor award, it was huge for me then, especially since Dr. Ferguson and Professor Moyer selected the awardee. Of course, I realize the award says nothing about how much improvement was needed!

Walking back to our table, I saw Dad wiping his eyes with a handkerchief. Dad had never been able to say he was proud of me. Although I learned he would take the ETSU Dean's List reported in the local newspaper to show his fellow workers, he just couldn't express his pride directly to me. And that was okay.

Graduating with honors and receiving congratulations and affirmations from the faculty was gratifying, but those old feelings of inadequacy and inferiority continued underneath. I had shown that the poor kid from McKinley Road could excel in polite society, but the question remained: where do I really belong?

The three years spent at Wesley Seminary were the most intense and transformative of my life. There, my view of God expanded. There, I learned to think theologically about life. There, I saw a vision of the church as an alternative to the world as it is. There, I was convinced that the church must engage the world and the crucial issues confronting humanity. There, I gained insight into my identity and began the ongoing process of being shaped by grace. There, I gained increased confidence by starting to integrate my background as a child of Appalachian poverty with God's claim upon my life. There, I made peace with fundamentalism by acknowledging that it contributed to my spiritual formation *and* left scars to heal. There, I experienced discipleship as being held and being held accountable. There, I began to see that God cares about the poor and those on society's margins. All previous boundaries of my Appalachian culture expanded.

But it was not only Wesley Seminary that accounted for the transformative nature of those three years. Serving as a student pastor was integral to the whole experience. Hunting Hill and MacDonald Chapel became partners in the formation process and enabled me to *do* ministry while reflecting *on* ministry. The dynamic relationship between theory and practice was lived out in ways that laid the foundation for the subsequent years of ministry.

A Student Pastor in the Washington Suburbs in the 1960s

Equally exciting to entering Wesley Seminary as a student was being appointed to the Hunting Hill and MacDonald Methodist Churches near Gaithersburg, Maryland. Surrounded by farmland, Gaithersburg was a small town of about five thousand on the edge of growing Washington suburbs. Two governmental agencies had recently located in the area, the National Bureau of Standards and the Atomic Energy Commission. When Linda and I arrived in June of 1962, Gaithersburg was not unlike small towns in East Tennessee, only closer to the bustle of urban D.C.

Hunting Hill and MacDonald Chapel were distinct congregations located two miles apart on Darnestown Road. Hunting Hill was a former Methodist Episcopal Church, founded around 1900, while MacDonald Chapel's heritage was the Methodist Episcopal Church, South, established a few years before Hunting Hill. Hunting Hill averaged approximately thirty-five in worship attendance, and MacDonald Chapel averaged around forty-five.

Hunting Hill's membership consisted largely of older members. Some were retired, some were farmers, and others were blue-collar workers. There were few children and youth. The congregation was all White and mostly middle class.

MacDonald Chapel consisted of similar demographics. A difference was many of its members were part of one family. Though MacDonald Chapel had few children and no organized youth group, there were more young adults than at Hunting Hill.

The two congregations became laboratories in my theological and pastoral formation, presenting opportunities for teaching, preaching, designing and leading worship, dealing with conflict, pastoral care amid crises, and organizing for mission. Preparing the congregations for the exponential growth in numbers and diversity of the population was a major challenge. The major focus was on building relationships between the congregations and responding to personal crises and struggles among the members. The boundaries of my own experience and abilities were constantly being stretched as relationships developed and integration of my poverty and emerging privilege continued.

Across the road from MacDonald Chapel was an old farmhouse covered with trees and vines that almost totally obscured it from view. The front of the house faced Darnestown Road and served as a country store run by Donald Snyder. Donald, his brother, Raymond, and Raymond's wife, Claudia, lived in the dilapidated house. I met Claudia on my first visit to the church. Upon arriving, I found the door unlocked. While walking toward the altar of the small, well-kept sanctuary, a squeaky voice came from near the pulpit, "Hello, hello." I saw no one. Again, I heard "Hello!" I responded with a hesitant "hello."

"I bet you are our new preacher. Go on up to the pulpit, and you will see the intercom. This is Claudia Snyder from across the road. I've been waiting for our new preacher to show up. Come across the road for a visit," she said.

I stepped into the pulpit and saw a small brown box through which Claudia listened to the services each week and sometimes talked to the congregation from her bed across the street. I then headed through the vines and bushes to the rustic, unpainted farmhouse. There, I found Claudia, blind and crippled with arthritis, confined to a bed in a dark, drab room. Beside the bed on a makeshift table made from soft drink cartons were the intercom, a telephone, a jar of peanut butter, and a partial loaf of bread. Tied to the railing at the foot of the bed was the rope she used to pull herself up. Claudia gripped the rope, sat up in bed, and extended her gnarled hand to her new preacher. She shared that each day, her husband, Raymond, positioned her in the bed with food and water on the table before departing to work in the fields on their nearby farm.

Claudia was one of the most positive, grace-filled people I have known. Though confined in a cramped, dimly lit room and unable to see colors or beauty, she seemed free, alive, and engaged. She immediately asked about me, and it felt like I was instantly one of the most important people in her life. She asked me to pray with her and to visit often. The telephone was placed beside her bed, not so much to ensure she could call in case of emergency, but rather because people called her, especially when they felt alone, distressed, or needed encouragement.

While in Tennessee for Christmas, I received a call that Donald had been shot in a robbery attempt on Christmas Eve. The robber entered the store and demanded money. Donald resisted by attacking the assailant with a fire poker, and he was shot. Linda and I cut short our holiday, and I had his funeral on New Year's Day in 1964, a major challenge for a twenty-four-year-old second-year seminary student.

Donald was educated as a lawyer and had accumulated considerable wealth, with large landholdings throughout Montgomery County, Maryland. He was considered an eccentric and never attended church. His brother, Raymond, inherited the wealth, but he and Claudia continued to live in cramped and bleak circumstances. Yet, Claudia seemed oblivious to her plight. She mourned Donald's death but never succumbed to vengeance or hatred.

Claudia died in the spring of 1965, and her funeral was my last one before returning to Tennessee. Raymond passed away a few years later, leaving an estate of extensive landholdings valued in the millions. Before his death, he gave a large gift to the county for a new hospital. The house and land across from MacDonald Chapel, bordering Quince Orchard Road and Darnestown Road, became the home of National Geographic. Today, it consists of shopping centers, office buildings, apartment and condo complexes, and upscale homes.

The relationship with the Snyder family influenced

my lifelong search for inner security in a world of economic and circumstantial uncertainty. Jesus' parable of the "foolish rich man" who built bigger barns to store his growing abundance as a means of security (Luke 12-13-31) has been a frequent text for sermons, as is the story of the rich man and Lazarus (Luke 16:19-31). As I review sixty years of ordained ministry, the dangers of wealth and privilege have been prevalent themes. The contrast between Claudia's inner peace and compassion for others and Donald's pursuit of security through accumulating wealth were dramatic portrayals of the ongoing tension between "the pawpaw patch" of Appalachian poverty and the world of increasing privilege and growing financial security.

Deeply embedded in me is a sense of solidarity with the vulnerable, such as Claudia. Like my mother, Claudia's strength came from within, and her compassion was without boundaries. Raymond's quiet, gentle manner and love for the land corresponded with Granddaddy Walker's core values. Added to my struggle was a growing awareness that the conflict between poverty and privilege was rooted in long-standing, systemic, socio-political problems. Where is the church in the struggle? Will my experiences in both worlds add to the problem or perhaps contribute in some small way to solutions? Little did I know these questions would tug at my conscience for a lifetime of ministry.

Conclusion

Historians describe the 1960s as one of the most transformative decades in world history. An editorial in *US News and World Report* called it "A Decade of Promise and Heartbreak." For me, 1962-65 were transformative years filled with unimagined shifts from the narrow margins of my racially segregated, religiously rigid, culturally provincial, economically impoverished, and educationally deficient background.

The distance between the world of the pushed-aside village of Watauga, Tennessee, and the privileged power center of the nation's capital could not be measured in miles. Little did Linda and I realize the life-transforming difference those three years would make when we drove into that new world over six decades ago.

Society's documented struggles and tensions of the 1960s were my internal personal challenges, the growing edges of my own worldview and values—confronting racism and White privilege, overcoming economic injustice and disparity, defining core values in a pluralistic world, engaging in theological exploration while remaining anchored in historic doctrines. Those tensions and challenges obviously were not resolved in those brief thirty-six months. However, the foundations were laid upon which ever-expanding opportunities and challenges could be met.

Those formative years propelled me *from*:

- A religion rooted in rules and fear *toward* a faith grounded in transforming GRACE.

- A gospel limited to personal *toward* a gospel that is personal, social, and communal.

- Salvation as transformation of hearts *toward* salvation as systemic and cosmic.

- A distant God of judgment *toward* an incarnate God of steadfast love.

- The church as a shelter from the world *toward* church as engagement with the world.

- Church as the center of God's mission *toward* church as a sign, foretaste, and instrument of Christ's present and coming reign of justice, compassion, generosity, and joy.

- Ministry as caring for the community *toward* ministry as shaping caring communities.

- Seminary as preparation for ministry *toward* theological education as a lifelong quest to know and share in the life and mission of the Triune God who is forever shifting the margins.

CHAPTER FOUR

Transitioning Back Home and a Changed World

The Calling of Home

Thomas Wolfe's novel *You Can't Go Home Again* was published posthumously the year I was born. Home for Wolfe—Asheville, North Carolina—is just across the mountain from my birthplace. The novel's protagonist, George Webber, leaves the confines of small-town Appalachia for a world of ever-expanding cultural, social, and personal frontiers. Though succeeding in the cosmopolitan centers of culture and power, "he always felt so strongly the magnetic pull of home."[3]

Though my sojourn into the tumultuous and exciting world beyond the hills of Appalachia was much shorter than George Webber's, the pull of home prevailed. The invitation to remain as pastor of the newly formed congregation in Maryland and the promise of nurturing a multi-racial congregation in a growing metropolitan area

---

[3] Thomas Wolfe, *You Can't Go Home Again* (New York: Harper & Row, 1940).

was tempting and lingers today as one of those "what ifs."[4]

Why this pull toward home with all its scars and wounds only partially healed? Could it have been a desire to prove myself to those with whom I felt inferior? Perhaps it was homesickness for family and friends. Did I think I could make a difference among the people and in the place that had birthed and nurtured me? Certainly, the conference leaders who ordained me deacon made me feel wanted. However mixed and mysterious the motives, home felt like a calling.

Parts of the world to which we were returning hadn't changed. The beautiful countryside looked the same. The small towns and homogeneous neighborhoods remained intact despite the Civil Rights Act of 1964 and growing racial conflicts in big cities. The "war on poverty" was more a dream than reality as poverty lurked across the tracks, on the back streets, and up the "hollers." Biblical literalism and fear-based apocalypticism still marked the religious landscape. A streak of anti-intellectualism and mistrust of educated "outsiders" ran deep. Economic disparity and exploitation had not diminished.

Yet, change was emerging. The nightly news, with its scenes of fighting in Vietnam and racial violence in our cities, disturbed the serenity of the once-peaceful neighborhoods and churches. The newborn optimism with the election of young President Kennedy present in 1960

---

[4] Hunting Hill and McDonald Chapel merged to form a new church and planned for inclusion of Pleasant View, a congregation in the segregated Central Jurisdiction.

had dissipated. War casualties in Southeast Asia were mounting, and young men were being drafted. Defeating the spread of "godless Communism" characterized much political discourse. The John Birch Society, founded in 1958, had reached a membership of approximately a hundred thousand by 1965, with local chapters in communities nationwide. Its claim to be based on Christian principles and a fierce anti-communist agenda laid a foundation for what is now the political and religious right. Conspiracy theories abounded, sowing widespread suspicion of the United Nations, the National and World Council of Churches, the civil rights movement, feminism, ecumenism, and liberalism.

Linda and I moved within ten miles of the riverbank community of Watauga that we had left only three years earlier. But home was different now. We were different. Every aspect of ME had changed or was in the process. My accent was different. I was speaking slower, putting ending consonants on words. Flat "i" was no longer flat. *Mountain* now included a "t." Theological naïveté had faded as reason and experience were incorporated into faith. Feelings of inferiority still lurked within, though now tempered with increased psychological insight and coping tools. My worldview had broadened beyond the provincial "pawpaw patch."

Can I go home again amid such personal and societal changes? Will I be accepted among kinfolks? Am I equipped to minister effectively in such a time as this? What changes are yet ahead? Will I be able to meet them with confidence, courage, and skill? The internal and external changes already in view were only intimations of the transformations awaiting. The stage was set for a lifetime of shifting margins, widening circles of relationships, expanding horizons, and deepening commitments to God's dream for home.

Vocational Calling Validated and Launched

In June 1965, I was received into full membership and approved for ordination as an Elder at the Holston Annual Conference session at Central Methodist Church in Knoxville. The presiding bishop was H. Ellis Finger, who was elected by the Southeastern Jurisdictional Conference in July 1964 while serving as president of Millsaps College in Jackson, Mississippi. His kind, stately demeanor, calm amid controversy, and humble competence immediately impressed me. Surprisingly, he introduced all the candidates for ordination with their full names without notes.[5] My appointment to Elizabeth Chapel in Bluff City, Tennessee, was announced at the conference.

Bishop Finger gave candidates for ordination the option of being ordained at annual conference or in their local church. While we were away in Washington, McKinley had merged with Tyner's Hill Methodist Church to form Fairhaven. I chose to be ordained in the local church,

---

[5] Bishop Finger had a remarkable gift for remembering names, endearing him to everyone. He and Mrs. Finger, Mamie Lee, became friends over the next fifty years. They were participants at Church Street UMC when I became pastor and, at their request, I did the homily at their funerals.

so my family and those who had nurtured me in the Methodist tradition could be present. On July 8, 1965, the small sanctuary was filled with family, former neighbors, and a few clergy colleagues who shared in the service and reception. John Bacon delivered the sermon since he was the pastor who had influenced me the most. Members of Elizabeth Chapel also attended to support their new pastor. I felt enormous support, affirmation, and excitement for ministry. And I felt at home!

Granny Walker was among those present. Though she had left the Methodist church and was suspicious of "educated preachers" and "the Conference," she was proud of her grandson. The service was relatively informal. We wore no robes, and the printed liturgy was minimal.

Admittedly, my awareness of the significance of the service was overshadowed by the many transitions taking place for me and Linda. Present were the tensions within me, the church, and society. My deep roots in rural Appalachian culture were embodied in my parents, Granny Walker, and most of the congregation. Bishop Finger, District Superintendent A. B. Wing, my college professor Robert Mielke, and colleague pastors personified the direction of my future.

Would I be able to remain connected to my roots while the horizons keep expanding and the privileges increase? Will my movement from poverty to privilege cut me off from the gifts of those who birthed and shaped me? Or will the gifts of those on the margins be central to how

I perceive and practice ministry with its accompanying privilege? Those questions/tensions/themes present that night have constantly pushed, pulled, and wooed me toward ever-shifting margins.

Part II

MINISTRY WITH THOSE ON THE MARGINS

CHAPTER FIVE

Poverty, Privilege, and Ministry

Stories of Economic and Spiritual Poverty

My background in economic poverty was kept a secret during my first four pastoral appointments. While I was embarrassed by my heritage, the family ties remained strong, and I felt drawn to connect with those like my family who were in the congregations and surrounding communities. Though they were increasingly on the margins of those churches, something kept enticing me toward them. I am not sure of the motives. Perhaps it was guilt for my increasing privilege. Maybe it was lingering insecurity in the presence of the more affluent and well-educated. Could it be that I felt superior in the presence of those on the margins? Where was God in all this?

Seminary had instilled the notion that every issue has theological components. The pastor's task is to identify, clarify, and bear witness to the theological vision related to issues confronting individuals and society. That formidable challenge requires rigorous study, prayer, and continuing conversation.

Following the advice of seminary professors and the challenge of Bishop Finger to keep a study regimen, I routinely spent four to five hours each morning studying. I read widely to keep abreast of emerging theological debates and trends, including the "death of God" debate, "situation ethics," and "process theology." My perspectives continued to develop, and I gleaned insights from various emerging theological currents. Liberation theology's notion that God has "a preferential option for the poor" was good news to me! It offered a framework within which to wrestle with personal struggles, not only with poverty but all forms of marginalization.

Lyndon Johnson's "war on poverty" and Robert Kennedy's tour of Appalachia brought to the forefront the disparities of wealth within our country. Though paternalism shaped much of the public rhetoric and policy discussions, the realities of poverty in America and its devastating consequences were widely exposed. Public images of Appalachia as portrayed on the evening news tended to reinforce negative stereotypes of ignorant "hillbillies," but the public was challenged to think more systemically about poverty and motivated to pursue a vision of "the Great Society." Surely, I thought, this is akin to the prophets' vision of justice and compassion for the poor and Jesus' proclamation of the "kingdom of God" where good news is proclaimed to the poor, release to the captives, sight is restored to the blind, the oppressed go free, and the year of jubilee justice comes to reality (Luke 4:18-19).

The deadly consequences of pervasive economic

disparity and injustice were at play in two painful pastoral situations at Elizabeth Chapel. Located near the church was a country store. The store owner's wife and children attended Sunday School regularly, though the father did not. Their house was attached to the store with a gas pump outside. The owner was kind, generous, and accommodating. He extended credit to almost anyone who asked, without keeping careful records. He often "rounded down" purchases, suggesting if something cost $1.10, "Oh, give me a dollar."

During a visit, he told me, "I'm going to lose the store, preacher! I can't pay my bills. I don't know what I will do. This is all I know, and my home is here, too. I just don't know what to do!" I had no solution. Then, he said, "If the people who owe me money would pay, I would be all right."

A few weeks passed, and I got a desperate call from his wife to come quickly. The store owner had died from suicide while the kids were in bed asleep. She wanted me to tell their three young children. How do you tell kids their dad is gone? I don't remember what I said. I just remember the tears, the hugs, the shared hurt. I was angry! I wanted to lash out at those who owed him money, some of whom listened each Sunday to my sermons. I refrained from unleashing my anger publicly and, at his funeral, called for compassion and generosity toward the family.

The store and house were auctioned a few weeks later to satisfy the indebtedness. Present and bidding on the property were two of the wealthier men in the community, one a church member. The deceased owner had named them to me as among the debtors.

A couple of years later, I received a call from the wife of a large landowner in the community. She said, "My husband has a brain tumor. He is in the hospital and has asked if you would visit him." Here was the man who exploited the poor of the neighborhood in his substandard rental houses lining the highway and who had contributed to and profited from the original store owner's death now asking me to visit him! I had to set my anger and condemnation aside. I prayed for calm and courage to make the visit.

I drove to the hospital, reflecting on what to do and say, asking for God's presence and direction. The patient greeted me with a gentle handshake and polite, "Thank you for coming, preacher." His summer tan had faded. The usual firmness in his eyes and steely determination in his face had given way to a forlorn, pleading countenance. Pity quickly allayed my anger. Compassion assuaged my judgmentalism. I said softly, "Your wife called. Thank you for inviting me to visit you. How are you feeling? How may I help?"

"I'm scared, preacher. My tumor is inoperable. There's nothing they can do." He added, "I've been blessed. Life has been good to me until now. I have everything and more than I ever dreamed of or needed. It's doing me no good now." Then he picked up a tiny piece of lint from his bedspread. "After all I have been given, this is more than I have given to the world," he said sadly as he held the lint between his index finger and thumb. Several visits followed before his death a few weeks later.

Why would those two incidents remain formative for the subsequent years of personal growth and leadership in ministry? These two men represented the tragic realities of economic inequality and the deadly consequences of injustice, greed, and exploitation. It became dramatically clear to me that spiritual poverty and economic poverty are intricately bound together, and the results are devastating to those seeking fulfillment in upward mobility, wealth, and control. Economic inequality, the interplay of theology and poverty, and the disconnect from the poor continue at the forefront of my own efforts to live and practice the Christian gospel.

Transitioning Out of Poverty into Privilege

The tension between my movement from the margins to the privileges of affluent society continued as I advanced up the institutional ladder. Linda and I epitomized the American dream. The birth of two lovely daughters, Sheri and Sandra, filled our lives with joy and added meaning. Though my income was modest, with the provision of parsonages and other benefits, we lived without economic struggles. Pastors were still respected in broader society, and the institutional church was at the zenith of statistical growth, especially in the suburbs as the growing middle-class White Americans moved from urban areas into subdivisions. Linda and I were among those enjoying the exodus from poverty to privilege. Yet, I could not escape the pull toward the margins.

After five years at Elizabeth Chapel, I was transferred thirty miles north to Pleasant View Church in Abingdon, Virginia. The congregation was transitioning from rural to suburban, with a growing number of young professional families. Our distance from the poor widened. None lived within view of the church! Any connection with those on the margins would have to be intentional.

It was 1970, and the "war on poverty" now included many local anti-poverty programs. The Peace Corps established by President Kennedy in 1961 had expanded to include domestic service. The Vietnam War was exacting more casualties, including a member of the congregation. Poverty and its victims were becoming more of an abstraction than a personal relationship, objects of the church's altruistic outreach rather than integral to its life.

It was one of those unexpected but seminal interruptions amid daily routine. A car drove into the parking lot outside my office while I was lost in preparation for Sunday's sermon. The young couple knocked on my door. After apologizing for showing up without an appointment, the young man introduced himself as Rees Shearer and his wife, Kathy. A colleague at Emory and Henry College had suggested they visit with me. Rees was a VISTA worker[6] in Georgia when he

---

[6] Volunteers in Service to America (VISTA) was a domestic version of the Peace Corps, established in 1965 as part of President Johnson's Economic Opportunity Act of 1964.

received his draft notice. As a conscientious objector and a citizen of Virginia, he had to return to Virginia and submit a plan within thirty days that would qualify as an alternative to military service. His passion for community organizing and development among people living in poverty was evident. He sought help in developing a plan to address poverty in the county.

I knew soliciting financial support and cooperation from local leaders would be challenging. Complicating the situation was the political climate in Washington County. VISTA workers had recently been expelled from the county, and a conscientious objector would not be readily accepted. Drawn to the Shearers' vision, I envied their commitment to living and serving among those suffering the consequences of poverty. What role could I play other than listening and encouraging Rees and Kathy and providing personal financial support?

Within the congregation were key leaders in the county, including the school superintendent, the welfare office director, and the county executive. Any program addressing systemic poverty would require the engagement of people with political clout and economic influence and power. They were in my congregation and neighboring churches. Marshaling the support of those influencers was now my opportunity and challenge. Herein, I discovered a critical component of ministry and the role of privilege: leveraging the power accompanying privilege for the benefit of the powerless.

Through the influence of Rees, Kathy, and others, I became increasingly active in community organizing efforts. I attended meetings of welfare rights organizations where I heard stories of people caught in the grip of unjust systems. I intentionally sat in on open AA meetings, taught a course at the local community college, visited the jail regularly, and met with clergy colleagues involved in social action efforts. My trusted pastoral relationships with people of power enabled me to win support for the Shearers and their vision. Though my inner struggle continued, the relationship with Rees and Kathy marked a critical turn in my journey from poverty to privilege. Perhaps my two worlds could be integrated.

Balancing activism, pastoral responsibilities, and ongoing study/education with family life was an unmet challenge. I worked compulsively. At one stretch, I went thirty consecutive days without a night off. Mealtimes and Saturdays were reserved for family, and we visited our parents about every two weeks. We managed short summer vacations, mostly at Linda's parents' cottage on Watauga Lake. Linda, Sheri, and Sandra were my refuge! But I always felt torn between spending time with them and the growing involvement with the church and engagement with those on the margins. It was only later that I was confronted with the personal and vocational consequences of my failure to resolve the ever-growing tension between my heritage in poverty and my increasing affluence.

In 1972, I was invited to preach at the Holston Annual Conference. Conference leaders decided that rather than inviting outside celebrities to preach, selected members of the conference would do the preaching. I was chosen as "a young pastor" to preach. Though I considered it a tremendous honor, I was scared. Would I fail and be exposed as an imposter? Do I really belong in such an arena? All those old haunting feelings of inferiority lurked in my mind.

Choosing the text of Mark 9:38-41, with the sermon entitled "The Danger of Labels," I described that amid the divisions between "conservatives" and "liberals," "evangelicals" and "social activists," so-called "patriots" and "communists," we miss the God who is working in those we dismiss as "the other." Without realizing it then, the sermon reflected the shifting margins active in my life and ministry. I called for a focus on deeds of compassion and justice as signs of God's coming kingdom. Seated to the side, visible in the corner of my eyes during the sermon, was Bishop L. Scott Allen, the first Black American bishop in the Southeastern Jurisdiction. His responses of "Amen," "Yes, Brother Carder," and "Preach it" were balm for my soul and stimulants for my confidence, as were smiles and nods from the congregation.

In 1973, I was appointed to Concord United Methodist Church in Knoxville, Tennessee. My appointment at age thirty-three to a rapidly growing congregation in the upscale suburbs of West Knoxville was not without controversy. Some older clergy colleagues saw it as damaging morale. It hastened the clash between the two worlds within my identity and vocation. Now I was living and serving among professional, highly educated, young, upwardly mobile families. I felt increasingly comfortable in that world and enjoyed the affirmation, prestige, and privileges accompanying the position. Yet, the sense of inferiority and the notion of being an imposter persisted. The unresolved tug between the world of McKinley Road and the suburbs of Knoxville manifested itself early.

Unresolved Scars Create a Barrier

About six months into the new appointment, the chairperson of the staff-parish relations committee, Sam Flanders, visited me. Sam was in his fifties, well respected, warm but straightforward in his conversations. "I wanted to come by for a chat and say that we really appreciate having you as our pastor. You are getting to know the congregation well, and we appreciate you and your beautiful family." Then followed that proverbial conjunction "But." My body tensed. I waited for the criticism to follow. I'm about to be exposed as an imposter. I'm not competent. I'm out of my league!

> *"But why are you angry at us when you preach?" asked Sam.*
>
> *"Angry? What do you mean, Sam?" I asked.*
>
> *"Often in your sermons, which are always well prepared, you seem angry, especially when you talk about money and wealth. I noticed it most in your recent sermon on 'The Dangers of Privilege.'"*
>
> *I was puzzled. "Sam, I didn't realize that. I'm not angry with you and the congregation."*

"You don't come across as angry in your relationships with us or when you teach classes. You're a good teacher and preacher. But sometimes, you seem to fuss at us when you preach."

Though the criticism hurt, I sensed his genuine concern and personal acceptance. I reviewed the manuscripts of my sermons, especially the one he referenced on privilege. Nothing in the manuscripts seemed especially accusatory or hostile. But listening to the cassette recordings, I heard the anger. There was an accusatory, bombastic tone in my voice.

Lindsey Grabeel was a neighbor, a member of the church, a psychiatrist, and the medical director of the Helen Ross McNabb Mental Health Center. I walked down the street for a friendly visit. I told him of the conversation with Sam and asked if he had detected anger. After confirming Sam's observation, Lindsey asked a direction-changing question: "How comfortable are you living in this affluent neighborhood? I'm interested in how you grew up." After briefly sharing my story, Lindsey remarked, "I wonder if the anger is toward yourself rather than us."

Yes! I was projecting anger at myself for my advancing privilege and growing affluence, which I was now enjoying. I was desperately trying to prove that I belonged among the successful and professional while running from hidden scars of poverty and cultural marginalization. My perfectionism and emerging workaholism threatened my emotional well-being and vocational effectiveness.

Months of personal reflection, conversations with

Linda, individual and group counseling, and clergy support group sessions followed. Self-disclosure in sermons and teaching sessions became more prominent, and the congregation began to learn of my heritage. Surprisingly, many of them shared similar backgrounds and the same struggles. I began to see my heritage as an asset rather than a liability.

The content of sermons regarding the dangers of wealth and privilege changed little. However, the spirit in which they were preached changed from condemnation to confession, from bombastic to invitational. Through the painful process, I learned that pastors are called to be pastorally prophetic and prophetically pastoral. The struggle and tensions did not totally dissipate, but I remained at Concord for ten years. I shudder to think what would have happened if Sam had not confronted me or if I had become defensive and denied the validity of the criticism.

Using Prosperity and Privilege for the Common Good

As my Appalachian heritage became less a source of embarrassment to be denied and more an asset to be properly used, I was liberated to use privilege as a resource for change. Nevertheless, the inner tension between my growing economic security and the plight of the poor remained. Now the tension is a source of constant self-reflection and a restraint against the perils of privilege. Keeping that tension alive requires intentionality in relationships and exposure to people affected by economic disparities. It means practicing generous stewardship of economic resources and professional influence. Relationships with people living in poverty, addressing economic injustices and disparities, practicing generous stewardship, and forming congregations of justice became central to subsequent ministry as a pastor and bishop.

Will Campbell, an iconoclastic Baptist preacher and civil rights advocate from Amite County, Mississippi, played an important role in my transition and formation.[7] He spoke to an ecumenical group of pastors in Knoxville in the mid-1970s on "The Suburban Captivity of the Church." After sharing the story of Vanderbilt Divinity School's practice of having ministerial students visit the "redlight district" of Nashville to test their call to ministry, Will remarked, "Hell, surviving Printers Ally is no test of your call to ministry! The real test is, 'Can you survive Sequoya Hills!'"[8] Ironically, fifteen years later, I would live in a parsonage in Sequoya Hills! His challenge marked a continuing struggle for me and the church: can we survive the temptations of growing privilege?

The answer lies in how we view our privilege, how privilege affects our relationships with those without privilege, and the use we make of the power accompanying privilege. I was determined to stay in personal relationships with those who live in poverty and to use my privilege as a means of addressing systemic and personal poverty.

---

[7] An article describing the influence of Will Campbell on my life: https://faithandleadership.com/ken-carder-bubba-gadfly-remembering-will-d-campbell.

[8] An upscale community in Knoxville.

My appointment in 1988 to Church Street, the "cathedral church" of Methodism in East Tennessee, brought into sharp focus the challenge of Will Campbell. Can I survive Sequoya Hills and remain in relationship with and committed to those marginalized by poverty and economic disparity? Can an economically affluent and socially/religiously prestigious congregation be in ministry with those who live in poverty?

The church is in downtown Knoxville, bordered on the west by the University of Tennessee. The business district with the courthouse, banks, governmental buildings, commercial offices, and arts centers is within walking distance to the east. To the south is the Tennessee River, and to the north at the time were the leftovers from the 1982 World's Fair. The large gothic sanctuary, with its stained-glass windows and towering spire, dominates the landscape.

The membership was predominantly affluent, professional White Americans. Many lived in the suburbs and drove into the city for work and church. The worship liturgy reflected the architecture—majestic and formal. The grand pipe organ and large, well-trained choirs made for exceptional musical contributions to worship and the arts. All the accruals of privilege were present.

But that's not the full story. Church Street is known and appreciated by those who live in poverty. Two longstanding ministries characterized the congregation's commitment: a soup kitchen that provided meals every Thursday to more than a hundred low-income and homeless persons and a multi-faceted tutoring and educational ministry in a low-income community across the river. When I arrived, a creative and passionate associate pastor, James Bailes, provided outstanding leadership of the church's presence with the people who visited the soup kitchen. He knew each by name, considered them friends, and was present *with* them. He set the tone for all the volunteers who treated each person with warm hospitality, deep respect, and God-given dignity. Many of the people arrived hours before lunch. They were treated as honored guests, and Jim often informally shared stories from scripture and engaged in humorous banter. During the week, several among the Thursday group stopped by the church, drank coffee, and chatted with whomever was available.

Through the soup kitchen, I got to know "Chief," Royetta, Richard, Ken, Tim, Rob Roy, Richard, Bill, Carroll, April, Byron, and many other friends. I heard their stories, laughed at their jokes, listened to their struggles, and learned from their insights. They were no longer "the poor" who came to the soup kitchen and objects of charity. They were friends and colleagues with a mutual longing for respect, love, and belonging. I looked forward to being with them and yearned to incorporate them into the total life of the congregation.

Traditionally, two Advent celebrations were held on successive Sunday afternoons, one for Church Street families and another for "families from the community," meaning those from the soup kitchen and from across the river. The question was raised as to why there were two separate celebrations. It felt exclusive and contradictory to the meaning of the Christmas Story. Would not this be an opportunity for us to embody the message of the Incarnation? After all, God came among us as an infant, born among the homeless, of a teenage, unwed mother.

The result was the "Community Christmas" held on Sunday afternoon in mid-December. Activities included making craft items as gifts, sharing an informal meal, and singing carols. The evening concluded with an unrehearsed enactment of the Nativity. With a supply of bathrobes, cardboard crowns, wrapped magi gifts, and white angel capes, participants were given the choice of being shepherds, magi/kings, and angels. The motley participants entered as the stories from Luke and Matthew were read. It was a glorious scene, a glimpse of heaven! Black and White angels, adult and children shepherds, university professors and homeless men as magi/kings together.

Shifting from viewing people who live in poverty as *objects of charity* to *friends in community* remained the challenge. The power/privilege differential remained obvious and insurmountable. Only a few of those hosted in the soup kitchen and "Community Christmas" attended Sunday worship. The gothic sanctuary with vaulted ceilings, stained glass windows, and stationed pews was a foreign, intimidating world for those living under the Henley Street Bridge or in a nearby shelter. The printed bulletins and scripted liturgy were embarrassing threats to those with minimal education. Their guitars, harmonicas, and whistling lips couldn't compete with the imposing sound of three thousand pipes playing a Bach toccata.

Jim Bailes suggested that it is unrealistic for us to expect those who come to the soup kitchen to feel comfortable in "our Sunday morning world." Perhaps we should be intentional in entering *their* world. They felt at home in the fellowship hall on Thursday. Why not design and conduct a service with people from the soup kitchen serving as the "hosts" and the Sunday morning Church Street attendees being the "visitors."

Jim's rapport with the people across socio-economic barriers and his theological grounding made the service possible. Though the attendance was small—usually less than fifty—participants crossed the socio-economic barriers. Gifts of the people living in the shelters and low-income housing were used in the service. Harry played his harmonica. Another played "the spoons." Participants selected hymns. They learned a new one, "God of the Sparrow, God of the Whale,"[9] which became a favorite. "Chief" often shouted, "Let's sing that whale song!" The text and tune capture a deep, universal longing for a God who cares for us amid all the stages and circumstances of living, whatever our social status.

On a cold Thursday evening in January, a stranger showed up for the service. Snow had fallen earlier in the week, and the ground remained frozen. As Jim and I greeted the people, we noticed the barefooted stranger. What was he doing here without shoes on a cold night

---

[9] "God of the Sparrow, God of the Whale," *The United Methodist Hymnal* (The United Methodist Publishing House), 122.

like this? Where could we get him some shoes? While the service was underway with singing, Jim and I made calls, and all the stores were closed. Still uncertain what to do, we returned to the fellowship hall. Surprisingly, the stranger was now wearing shoes! Looking around the room, we realized Rob Roy was now barefoot. He had given his shoes to the stranger! He said, "It's no big deal. I've got another pair at the shelter."

It never occurred to me to give the stranger my shoes! I had several pairs in the closet at home, and I would ride home in my warm car. One to whom the sting of poverty was a present reality intuitively, without fanfare, simply responded compassionately to a stranger without shoes. Despite efforts otherwise, my privilege removed me from solidarity with those without privilege. I saw the stranger's need and wanted to find a solution *outside* myself. I moved immediately to a charitable solution. I only saw the stranger as a person with no shoes. I never learned his name! Rob Roy saw him as a person. He learned his name. They were brothers, friends, equals. I suspect the stranger accepted Rob Roy's shoes with his dignity intact, not resentfully as an object of patriarchal charity. The incident taught me a lot about grace.[10] It also reminded me of my childhood experience when I was treated as an object of charity, and it confirmed that the opposite of poverty isn't wealth; it is dignity.[11]

---

[10] I used this incident in a lecture delivered at a symposium on Theology and Evangelism in the Wesleyan Tradition in 1992. The lecture is included in James C. Logan, editor, *Theology and Evangelism in the Wesleyan Heritage* (Kingwood Press, 1994), 81-94.

[11] I first heard a similar statement made by Mvume Dandala, a leader in the Methodist Church of Southern Africa, whom I met in 1995 while visiting South Africa.

Theological Foundation and Vision Strengthened and Expanded

It may seem paradoxical that the theological foundation and vision for presence with those on the margins, especially the poor, deepened during my four years living in Sequoya Hills and serving the "cathedral church." An unexpected assignment from the denomination contributed to the wedding of Wesleyan theology with my own pastoral practice.

As a delegate to General Conference in 1988, I was assigned to the legislative committee on faith and order, which was tasked with reviewing, amending, and recommending the committee report from the 1984 General Conference on the revised doctrinal statement. The document, "Doctrinal Standards and Our Theological Task," was overwhelmingly adopted. A few months after the General Conference, I was invited to write *The Leaders' Guide for Our Doctrinal Standards and Theological Task* for the newly approved statement. I was honored, humbled, and afraid, but accepted the challenge.

Preparation for writing the *Leaders' Guide* required immersion in Wesley's life and writings. John Wesley's relationships with the poor of eighteenth-century England became evident, though that aspect of the Wesleyan tradition had received no emphasis in my previous study. It became evident that Wesley's life, theology, and ministry were influenced significantly by his relationships with those on the margins, especially the poor and those in prison.

The convergence of pastoral ministry, theological

integration, institutional leadership, relationships with and commitment to people living in poverty, and personal privilege dominated my tenure at Church Street. My increased familiarity with John Wesley gave me a broader theological lens and a greater confidence in my role.

Wesley's robust concept of universal grace transforming human hearts, communities, nations, and the entire cosmos provided a theological foundation and vision of holistic salvation. Grace unites the personal and the social, piety with education and knowledge, and even privilege with poverty. Wesley's privileged life became instrumental in his ministry. Though privileged blind spots remained, his love for, presence with, and ministry on behalf of those on the margins of eighteenth-century England were visible signs, foretastes, and instruments of God's present and coming reign of compassion, justice, hospitality, generosity, and joy. May it be so in my own life and ministry!

A New Challenge with Greater Privilege, Greater Opportunity, and Greater Temptation

At the 1991 session of the Holston Annual Conference, I was elected to lead the delegation to the 1992 General Conference. At the meeting of the delegation, the question of endorsing an episcopal candidate was considered. Based on precedent, the clergyperson elected first would be considered. In anticipation of being considered, I talked with colleagues and Bishops Finger, Lee, and Eutsler. Linda remained my primary conversation partner and leaned toward me being considered.

Should I permit my name to be submitted? It was an unparalleled compliment that stroked my brittle ego! But was it my calling? Could I fulfill the duties if elected? Lurking deep within were the gnawing doubts and questions of motives: Am I genuinely open to the call of God through the church, or is it my need for approval through gaining prestige? Is my catapulting privilege a gift to be used on behalf of those on the margins, or was it but a clever manipulation of institutional processes and positions? Underlying motives are always mixed, and I can never claim purity of intention. Whatever the motives, I acquiesced to the election process.

Several events and responsibilities had put my name before the wider constituency in the denomination. The dialogue between the bishops and leaders of the nuclear industry in Oak Ridge had received wide publicity.[12] I chaired a General Conference task force on genetic science and ethics, which garnered church and secular press coverage. *The Leaders' Guide* was being used by pastors across the denomination, and I had written a few articles for *Circuit Rider* and *Engage Magazine*.

The Jurisdictional Conference elected me on July 17, 1992. I was escorted to the stage by Bishops Clay Lee and Kern Eutsler; Linda was escorted by Bishop Ellis Finger, along with our daughters. Dad and Mom were present. The

---

[12] With the encouragement and assistance of Bishop Eutsler, I worked with local church leaders to arrange the dialogue. Sixteen bishops participated in the two-day conversation. As the pastor, I served as host and facilitator.

presiding bishop, Ernest Newman, took the extraordinary action of requesting that my parents be brought to the stage. What a gift! I embraced them with "I love you" as the congregation applauded. In those few minutes, a family from the margins was celebrated. One was welcomed at the center of the denomination's power and privilege.

The consecration service for newly elected bishops concluded the Jurisdictional Conference. As the bishops and worship leaders lined up for the procession, a bus arrived in front of Stuart Auditorium at Lake Junaluska, North Carolina. It was filled with people from Church Street, including friends from the soup kitchen and the Thursday evening worship service. As they stepped off the bus and made their way toward the auditorium, they spotted me and waved enthusiastically, attracting the attention of the robed bishops and worship leaders. "Who are those folks, Ken?" asked the curious bishops. "They are my friends," I responded proudly. It was obvious from their dress and demeanor that they were not the typical attendees at the consecration service of new bishops in a predominantly middle-class church. One account reported the group who arrived to support newly elected Bishop Ken Carder "looked like a circus."

Such a characterization both angered and gladdened me. That the very people who were at the center of Jesus' life and ministry would be viewed as out of place on such an occasion smacked of elitism and lost mission. Their presence dramatized the marginalization of the poor by the institution whose mission is to "bring good news to the poor." Those whom Charles Wesley called "Jesus' bosom friends" were a sideshow, a circus, among the privileged leaders of the institution claiming loyalty to the Wesleyan tradition. Yet, their presence kindled a sense of gratitude for my heritage, their friendship, and a renewed sense of stewardship of the privilege being bestowed. This concluding charge to the newly consecrated bishops became my challenge and opportunity:

> *Be to the people of God*
> *a prophetic voice and courageous leader*
> *in the cause of justice for all people.*
> *Be to the flock of Christ a shepherd;*
> *support the weak, heal the sick,*
> *bind up the broken, restore the outcast,*
> *seek the lost, relieve the oppressed.*
> *Faithfully administer discipline,*
> *but do not forget mercy,*
> *that when the Chief Shepherd shall appear*
> *you may receive the never-fading crown of glory. Amen.*[13]

The next few weeks were filled with transitions, both exciting and frightening. Linda and I were thrilled to be assigned to the Nashville Area, which included the Tennessee and Memphis Conferences. We returned to Knoxville and hurriedly prepared to move to Nashville, where I would assume episcopal duties on September 1. Church Street members greeted our election with a sense

---

[13] *The United Methodist Book of Worship* (The United Methodist Publishing House, 1992), 706.

of pride and expressed disappointment. Although I felt highly honored and inspired by the new direction, I also had a gnawing sense that I was leaving prematurely.

Months earlier, I had committed to attend the Ninth Oxford Institute of Methodist Theological Studies at Sommerville College, Oxford. Gathering with Wesley scholars and church leaders from around the world proved to be an appropriate shift from local to global leadership in the denomination. It also provided time for Linda and me to adjust to the expanded scope of our life together. The Institute's theme, "Good News to the Poor in the Wesleyan Tradition," captured the growing edge of my theology and vision of the church's mission. Theodore Jennings delivered the keynote address: "Wesley and the Poor: An Agenda for Wesleyans."[14] Little did I realize that his address would set the agenda for my first two quadrennia as a bishop and that Ted and I would become close friends and colleagues in pursuing that agenda.

An Episcopal Initiative – Children and Poverty

During my first meeting of the Council of Bishops, the question of an Episcopal Initiative was on the agenda. All bishops were encouraged to offer suggestions, including the sixteen new members of the council. The tradition of new bishops remaining silent had been put aside in recent years, and Council president Joe Yeakel intentionally

---

[14] Theodore Jennings' book, Good News to the Poor: *John Wesley's Evangelical Economics* (Abingdon Press, 1990), contributed significantly to my understanding of John Wesley.

involved "rookie" bishops in the discussions. I felt compelled to suggest that the Council address poverty as an Episcopal Initiative. Two other suggestions were the environment/climate and children. In support of my suggestion, I referred to the theme of the Oxford Institute, which several other bishops attended. No consensus emerged, so Bishop Yeakel appointed task forces to further explore the suggested themes.

Surprisingly, I was appointed to chair the task force on poverty. We were asked to help the Council address poverty from a Wesleyan perspective. I immediately invited Ted Jennings to serve as a consultant. Over the subsequent months, the task group challenged Council members to establish personal relationships with people living in poverty and to covenant with one another to donate any increases in salary during the quadrennium to aid the poor. The responses were mixed. Though both proposals were adopted, they were deemed voluntary, and no mechanism was in place to hold one another accountable to implement them.

The Council was slow in selecting an Episcopal Initiative. The decision was finally made in 1996 to declare "Children and Poverty" as the Initiative. The initial arguments for prioritizing children focused on the decline of children in Sunday School. We pointed out that the children who need priority consideration are those living in poverty. Keeping the focus on economic poverty remained a challenge.

The Task Force on the Episcopal Initiative was formed with Bishop Jack Meadors serving as chairperson and me as secretary. Using input from the task force and theological consultants Pamela D. Couture and Theodore Jennings, I was asked to write the foundation document, describing the problem being addressed, the theological grounding for addressing the problem, and the goals for the initiative.

The primary goal of the Episcopal Initiative was stated:

Nothing less than the reshaping of The United Methodist Church in response to the God who is among "the least of these" is required. The evaluation of everything the Church is and does in the light of the impact on children and the impoverished is the goal. The anticipated result is the development of forms of congregational and connectional life and mission that will more faithfully reflect and serve the God revealed in Jesus Christ. Communities of faith shaped by God's presence with the most vulnerable represent alternatives to the values and visions of the prevailing culture.[15]

The foundation document was approved and distributed throughout the denomination. The impact of the Initiative depended on the bishops' leadership in their episcopal areas and varied widely among the bishops. The Nashville Area responded positively. Implementing the Initiative became a priority in both the Tennessee and Memphis Conferences. It became understood throughout the conference that

---

[15] "Children and Poverty, AN EPISCOPAL INITIATIVE: Biblical and Theological Foundations," The Council of Bishops of The United Methodist Church, 1996.

"the bishop's priority" was ministry with people living in poverty. Wesley Seminary and the two conferences developed a Doctor of Ministry track on "Wesley and the Poor," with fourteen of our pastors enrolling.

The episcopal office was relocated from the suburbs to downtown Nashville in the historic McKendree United Methodist Church, where we would be closer to the homeless and within walking distance of centers of economic and governmental activity. The old Ryman Theatre, the former home of the "Grand Ole Opry," was now within view of my office window, a sign of the "pawpaw patch" from my Appalachian roots.

The ambitious goals were never reached, but the Initiative remained a part of the Council of Bishops' efforts until 2004, when a class of twenty-four new bishops entered the Council. Some newly elected bishops led efforts to set aside the plans adopted by the Council in the spring of 2004 which called for the Council to prioritize in the new quadrennium the vision of "the Beloved Community" as the next step in the Initiative on Children and Poverty and to implement the recommendations contained in the Episcopal Address delivered at the recent General Conference.[16]

The discussion within the Council was intense! Some newly elected bishops argued that they were elected to help

---

[16] The Council selected me to deliver the Episcopal Address, "The New Creation and the Mission of the Church." It included a commitment by the bishops to lead the Church in embodying "the new creation" and a study of foundational themes in Wesleyan theology and practice. The response was mixed, and the address fell short of inspiring the denomination toward a compelling vision.

change the direction of the denomination. They intended to lead the Council in advancing the mission statement approved by the General Conference of 2000: "to make disciples of Jesus Christ." Their arguments centered on reversing the decline in membership, and the focus was clearly on the institutional church and away from the world the church exists to serve.

I reasoned that God's preoccupation is the world's needless suffering, violence, and injustices, not membership declines in The United Methodist Church. The counterclaim was that the church needs to be institutionally strong to respond to the world's suffering. The question was raised: for what purpose do we make disciples of Jesus Christ? "In order to transform the world" emerged as the answer. Therein birthed the addition to the mission statement that was revised at the 2008 General Conference at the request of the Council: the mission of the Church is "to make disciples of Jesus Christ for the transformation of the world."[17] The addition of the phrase reflects a political compromise within the Council rather than a clearly defined theological/missional vision. The priority focus shifted to the institutional church, with the suffering of the world, at best, relegated to a secondary emphasis.

---

[17] The phrase "for the transformation of the world" was used by the bishops throughout the 2004-2008 quadrennium when discussing the mission of the church. At the 2008 General Conference, the mission statement was revised to read: "The mission of the Church is to make disciples of Jesus Christ for the transformation of the world." *The Book of Discipline of The United Methodist Church* (The United Methodist Publishing House, 2016), 93.

Advocacy and Public Policy

My personal energies related to poverty shifted to advocacy and addressing systemic issues and public policy. One of the first ecumenical and community-wide speaking invitations was to address the annual "Legislative Prayer Breakfast," which included pastors, judicatory leaders, legislators, the governor, and other "movers and shakers." I addressed the use and abuse of power, using the story of Elisha in 2 Kings 2:23-25. The prophetic mantle had just been passed from Elijah to Elisha with the accompanying power and prestige. He quickly used his newly acquired power to purify the water system for the city of Jericho. But as he was leaving the city and traveling to Bethel, some small boys jeered at him, "Go away, baldhead! Go away, baldhead!"

Surveying the room, I saw several men with little or no hair, including Governor Ned McWherter. Pointing to my bald head, I whimsically suggested that I empathize with Elisha, but his reaction to a personal insult was a gross abuse of power. He called out "two she bears" who mauled the boys! I suggested we are all tempted to use power to resolve personal grievances and identity issues. However, power is to be exercised on behalf of justice and the common good, adding that justice in the Judeo-Christian tradition requires enabling the least and most vulnerable to flourish, "the orphans, widows, and sojourners" and "the least of these."

The ten-minute speech had far-reaching results. Present

were future friends, ecumenical colleagues, and political allies. An organized group of judicatory leaders emerged shortly thereafter, consisting of Catholic and Episcopal bishops, the Presbytery moderator, a United Church of Christ executive, and a Jewish rabbi. We met regularly to discuss wide-ranging issues facing the city and state. Trust developed over the intervening months and years.

Relationships emerged with key political leaders, including Representative Bill Purcell, an active United Methodist who was majority leader and chair of an important legislative committee on children and youth. He later became mayor of Nashville.[18] Another ally was Gordon Bonnyman, an attorney who worked for legal services and represented low-income individuals. He and his wife, also an attorney, founded the Tennessee Justice Center in 1995, a nonprofit law firm devoted to advocacy and service on behalf of low-income families.

When the Tennessee governor and General Assembly began to address "welfare reform" in the mid-1990s, we met as religious leaders to offer input. We enlisted the advice of Gordon Bonnyman and Representative Purcell as to the most effective ways to impact legislation. Representative Purcell invited us to testify before his committee and suggested we arrange a meeting with the new Republican governor, Don Sundquist. Both

---

[18] William (Bill) Purcell was elected mayor of Nashville in 1999. He asked me to gather the religious leaders together and meet with him once each month to "hold me accountable to my promises and integrity of leadership." We covenanted that those meetings would be "off the record."

Bonnyman and Purcell suggested that childcare was a major component of the "Families First" legislation being proposed by Governor Sundquist and the Republicans since they were advocating "welfare to work" as the core of their proposals.

As religious leaders, we agreed that solidarity with those affected by the legislation/policy would be important, and our first step was to identify the commonly held core theological/ethical principles that should shape the legislation. These emerged from our discussion:

- All persons are created in the image of God with inherent worth and dignity, and all policies adopted must respect the worth and dignity of all.

- A primary criterion of justice is enabling the least and most vulnerable to flourish as beloved children of God made in the divine image, which requires access to the necessities for a fulfilling life, including food, shelter, education, and medical care.

- Legislation and public policy must prioritize compassion and justice over protecting the privileges of the already privileged.

A meeting with Governor Sundquist and his staff was arranged to offer input into the "Families First" legislation. Following introductions, I thanked the governor for the meeting and for his commitment and leadership in efforts to reform the welfare system. "As leaders of diverse faith communities across the state, we are committed to working with you where possible in improving the lives of our fellow citizens, especially the most vulnerable," I stated. We then presented a copy of the above principles as our agreed-upon guidelines for evaluating all legislative proposals. Rabbi Kanter emphasized that central to both Judaism and Christianity is God's preferential concern for "the orphans, widows, and sojourners," the poor and most vulnerable. We asked if the governor agreed with the principles to which he gave assent.

We politely told the governor we intended to be constructive without being co-opted or used for political advantage. Our preference was to work cooperatively without publicity and that we will be direct with our suggestions. However, we declared that we would be open and public with opposition to proposals that violate the agreed-upon principles. We specifically identified inadequate support for childcare as a concern since the governor's proposal was significantly below the average cost across the state.

The governor proposed that a representative of the faith communities be present at each advisory board meeting and that we continue the conversations, which we did. A tangible result was the raising of the amount allowed for childcare, though it still fell short of our goals.

Maintaining personal relationships with people on the margins while focusing on advocacy and systemic issues required intentionality. Sustained friendships with the poor became almost impossible. I was able to establish personal relationships with a few who lived in poverty. Norman, a member of Good Samaritan Church in Memphis, a recovering addict who had lived on the streets but now worked with at-risk kids in the inner city, became a friend. He called my office often and simply left a message, "Tell the bishop I love him." Another was Vivian, a member of 61st Avenue United Methodist Church in the industrial section of West Nashville. All members of the congregation were on public assistance. I often visited the church and attended the Saturday evening worship service occasionally. I met Vivian at the reception when I first arrived as bishop in Nashville. Amid the reception's formality, she gave me a big bear hug and said, "Welcome, Bish!" She showed up at several meetings, greeted me with the same robust hug, and said, "I love you, Bish!"

Edgehill Church and the pastor, Bill Barnes,[19] were also anchors. Bill, a graduate of Yale Divinity School, was the founding pastor and an activist for racial and economic justice. The church is strategically located between Vanderbilt University, United Methodist agency buildings, and public housing. It was/is a Reconciling Congregation, openly welcoming of LGBTQ people, multi-racial, and socio-economically diverse. When Bill came to me in 1995 to announce his intention to retire, I shared my envy of his ability to live in both worlds of privilege and poverty, always maintaining personal relationships with people on the margins. I made the tongue-in-cheek comment that I was tempted to appoint myself to Edgehill and resign the episcopacy. His serious response helped maximize

---

[19] See Reverend Bill Barnes, *To Love a City: A Congregation's Long Love Affair with Nashville's Inner City* (private printing).

my use of privilege: "Don't you dare consider leaving the episcopacy. You've been put in that office by the church, and that gives you a place at tables of power that I will never have. The poor and powerless need you there! That's your calling now. You are there on our behalf."

Practicing responsible stewardship of privilege lies at the heart of leadership and Christian discipleship. Such stewardship requires keeping alive the inner tension between one's own privilege and systemic poverty and resisting the ever-present temptation to root identity in socio-economic status. The market logic of capitalism in which we live suggests that our worth and security lie in what we own or produce or the ability to control others. In such an environment, the Jesus way of self-emptying love and solidarity with the poor and the powerless is countercultural. Living Jesus' way involves constant repentance, intentional personal friendships with the poor, generous sharing of wealth, and challenging exploitive systems designed to protect the privileges of the privileged rather than creating systems that welcome ALL people at God's table of abundance.

Conclusion

Prosperity, power, and privilege are pervasive gods competing for dominance over self-emptying love, human solidarity, and universal flourishing. The struggle is personal and social, spiritual and structural, relentless and redemptive. The following are shifts in my continuing struggle:

- Poverty viewed as purely economic *toward* poverty seen as theological and spiritual realities
- Prosperity, power, and privilege as measures of identity and worth *toward* responsible stewardship of position and influence
- The poor and powerless as objects of charity *toward* friendship, solidarity, and mutuality
- Ministry and mission-focused within the church *toward* enabling connection to God's presence and mission in the world
- The worlds of poverty and privilege as barriers *toward* integration and tension as a means of growth and maturity

CHAPTER SIX

Confrontation with Personal and Institutional Racism

Race Beyond an Abstraction

Race was an abstraction in my early years. The county I grew up in had only twenty-five hundred Black Americans, less than four percent of the total population. Segregated schools, churches, and sports teams afforded no opportunity for friendships across racial lines. I saw "Whites Only" signs at drinking fountains and lunch counters. The "N-word" was common. Segregation was just "the way things are." We breathed the air of White superiority, and poor White Americans ranked higher in social status than those labeled "colored." News of racial strife and civil rights appeared on the news, but that took place elsewhere.

I read *Harriet Beecher Stowe's Uncle Tom's Cabin* in the eighth grade and mentioned it to my mother. In her characteristic empathy, she bemoaned the cruelty of slavery. In high school and college, references to race were confined to noncritical historical references to the Civil War, with some teachers questioning whether the war was about slavery. Systemic racism and critical race theory hadn't yet reached academia. No references to racial prejudice and injustice were heard in church.

The boundaries within my White-dominated world began to expand with the move to Maryland in 1962. The margins shifted as friendships formed with Black American students whose stories personalized the deadly consequences of personal prejudice and systemic racism. Race ceased to be an abstraction and became a personal encounter. The church plays a significant role in confronting my own racial prejudices and participation in systemic racism.

Early Exposure to Systemic Racism within the Church

Within sight of MacDonald Chapel was Pleasant View Methodist Church. Pleasant View members were Black Americans and, therefore, part of the Central Jurisdiction, a racially segregated structure instituted when the Methodist Episcopal Church and the Methodist Episcopal Church, South, united in 1939. Within two miles on the same busy highway were the visible expressions of the racial and regional divide within The Methodist Church—a former Methodist Episcopal Church; Methodist Episcopal Church, South; and the Central Jurisdiction. The Pleasant View membership was small, and the buildings included a sanctuary and an adjacent fellowship hall. A Black American neighborhood was hidden off the main road, and a few Black Americans lived in new subdivisions in nearby Rockville.

While driving past Pleasant View, I spotted a man walking toward a parked car. I stopped and introduced myself. "I'm Tom Barrington, the pastor here," was his response. I learned he was also the pastor of a church with three hundred members in another community. He was in his mid-fifties and a seminary graduate. He grew up in North Carolina and moved north for school and to escape the segregation of his native state. Frequent conversations followed that brief encounter. Tom became my friend and teacher.

George Wallace was very much in the headlines with his resistance to integration. A few weeks earlier, on June 11, 1963, Governor Wallace stood in the doorway at the University of Alabama to block entry by two Black American students, Vivian Malone and James Hood.

"I don't have a lot of trouble with Wallace," said Barrington. "At least I know where I stand with him. To him, I am just a damn [N-word]. But to a lot of people around here, I don't know where I stand. They are polite and nice on the surface but still consider me a second-class citizen or worse."

As a twenty-two-year-old part-time student pastor with no experience, I learned that my annual salary was three hundred dollars *more* than this experienced pastor of two churches, one larger than Hunting Hill and MacDonald Chapel combined. I was benefitting from the inequalities within the Methodist Church as the salary systems were separate and unequal.

Members of MacDonald Chapel and Hunting Hill generally did not speak openly of prejudice toward Black Americans. Explicit expressions of prejudice were no longer socially acceptable. Yet, they had no personal relationships with the members of Pleasant View who lived in the same community, tucked away in a small enclave.

What began as a casual introduction and continued as sporadic encounters resulted in unexpected, unplanned, and ongoing consequences for the three congregations. During one conversation, Tom mentioned that some boys in his congregation were interested in becoming Boy Scouts. I innocently suggested that since Hunting Hill and MacDonald Chapel had a combined troop, youngsters from Pleasant View could join them. Tom, less naïve than I, suggested I had better check that out with my churches.

The scout leaders agreed to invite the Pleasant View kids to join the troop and suggested that a man from Tom's congregation serve as one of the leaders. I was delighted to report their enthusiastic support to Tom. He reacted with surprise. We did not realize it, but that marked the first step toward a new multi-racial church in Montgomery County!

Since the Methodist Men sponsored the troop, leaders suggested a joint "meet and eat" group with the men from Pleasant View. Nothing important took place—or did it? It's amazing how radical results are preceded by seemingly inconsequential, unnoticed decisions or events amid routine activities by simple, anonymous, powerless people long forgotten. Maybe that is what Jesus meant by parables of the kingdom, the seed and the leaven.

Shortly thereafter, the president of the Pleasant View women's group invited their counterpart from MacDonald Chapel to share a joint session. So, about a dozen women from each church gathered in the fellowship hall at Pleasant View. Although the women lived in the same community and were all Methodists, they were strangers.

The informal gathering time was cordial and pleasant, with both groups expressing some nervousness. As the women gathered, a member of MacDonald Chapel whispered to me, "I'm glad we're doing this. I've wanted to meet these women. I need someone to do my house cleaning. This could be a good opportunity to find someone." Was she in for a surprise!

As we took seats around the table, the chosen seating arrangement illustrated modeled segregation, MacDonald Chapel on one side and Pleasant View on the other. Participants introduced themselves by sharing names, family, and jobs. Guests from MacDonald Chapel were invited to go first. "I'm Mildred, and I'm a homemaker with five children," said one. Other jobs identified were telephone operator, secretary, clerk, and lab technician, but homemaker was the dominant response from my side of the table.

Then came the introductions from Pleasant View members: Howard University professor, NIH biologist, schoolteacher, and a couple of homemakers. All those who worked outside the home were professional women. Following the introductions, I leaned over to ask my member, "Did you find anyone to clean your house?" Fortunately, we had a good relationship, and she merely whispered, "I deserved that!"

Much to my surprise, the following program focused on "Race Relations." I was astounded that, for the first time, this small group of Black and White American women sat around a table and discussed race. It was a transformative gathering for the women from MacDonald Chapel.

It was the 1960s, yet the relationship with Pleasant View created minimal controversy. In fact, we seldom talked about it, and no issue ever arose from the scouts. It seemed no big deal that Black and White American boys were now gathering each week and going on camping trips together or that Black and White American neighbors—fellow Methodists—started talking with each other at the local service station or grocery store.

At a later meeting of the Hunting Hill/MacDonald Chapel and Pleasant View Methodist Men's Club, the feasibility of Pleasant View becoming involved in ongoing fellowship with the other two churches was formally discussed. The two men's groups agreed to be the catalyst for ongoing discussion of fellowship within the three congregations.

In the meantime, MacDonald Chapel and Hunting Hill merged to form a new congregation, Fairhaven Methodist. In Acts 2:7, Fair Havens was the harbor that Apostle Paul entered for renewal and repair on his journey to Rome.

Fairhaven seemed fitting for a church seeking to minister in the turbulent, changing waters of the 1960s and beyond—a place for renewal for continued engagement in mission.

In 1968, the Pleasant View membership voted to transfer its membership to Fairhaven. Interestingly, those three congregations became one the same year the Central Jurisdiction was dissolved, the Methodist Church merged with the Evangelical United Brethren Church, and The United Methodist Church was formed. Little did I realize then that the newly formed congregation, representing the history of the denomination's racial divisions, foreshadowed the hopes for the denomination.[20]

Backlash and Racial Tensions

Racial tensions ran high in 1965 when Linda and I returned to the South. Backlashes against the civil rights movement reached a boiling point with the murder of Martin Luther King, Jr., on April 4, 1968. Tensions were prevalent in personal conversations among church members and neighbors. The "N-word" was still acceptable in the predominantly rural community where we now lived, and interaction with Black people was rare. During worship the Sunday following the King assassination, I expressed admiration for Dr. King as "a modern-day prophet and one of the greatest men of the twentieth century." The pastoral prayer included

---

[20] Fairhaven United Methodist Church exists as a vital multi-racial congregation. See their website: https://www.fairhavenumcmaryland.com/.

thanksgiving for his witness and a petition that his dream would become a reality in our community and nation.

Following the service, a lay leader objected to my prayer and comments about "that damned Communist." During a subsequent conversation, I challenged his characterizing Dr. King as a "Communist." He disputed and claimed that J. Edgar Hoover had confirmed such a designation. I countered, "I don't think Hoover has made such a statement," and declared, "I'll write to him and ask." So I did. Surprisingly, within a month, a short response came from the FBI director: "I have never stated that Dr. Martin Luther King, Jr., was a Communist." I proudly showed him the letter. With a smirk, he retorted, "Well, Hoover only said that he had never *stated* he was a Communist. He didn't say he *wasn't* one." No argument was going to erase deep-seated racial prejudice. Thankfully, he and I remained friends despite such disagreements.

Experiences in seminary and as a student pastor sensitized me to the importance of personal relationships across racial barriers. I missed Tom Barrington, members of Pleasant View, and fellow seminary students who had challenged my prejudices and parochialism. I had returned to a segregated world. All neighbors were White. Monthly pastors' meetings included only White American clergy until the Central Jurisdiction ended three years after our move back to Tennessee. Since only a few Black American Methodist churches existed in the region, interactions with Black American pastors were rare. Yearning for such relationships, I contacted Amos Holmes, pastor of John Wesley Church in Bristol, Virginia.

Amos was a Georgia native, where he had served as pastor and been active in civil rights efforts. After Dr. King's death, he received an increasing number of harassing phone calls, creating anxiety for his family. The hostility he received made my unease over disagreements with parishioners seem petty. Amos' inner strength, quick wit, courage, and disarming humor had been honed over a lifetime of confronting discrimination and threats. He had an uncanny ability to deflect insults back on his attacker. For example, a man called late at night and said, "You're nothing but pile of sh-t! I'm going to come by your house and put a bucket of horse sh-t on your front porch!" Amos responded, "Well, thank you! Please add some of your own, and let me see if I can tell the difference!" Dial tone. The cold stares and suspicious whispering while sharing a public meal with Amos provided me a faint hint of what he and Black Americans endured persistently.

Growing Confrontation with Institutional Racism in the Church

The dissolving of the racially segregated Central Jurisdiction in the newly formed United Methodist Church in 1968 immediately impacted my home conference. L. Scott Allen, a Black American, became our bishop. Having learned the value of relationships in changing racial attitudes, I eagerly awaited the arrival of Bishop Allen and increased opportunities to form relationships across racial barriers.

Being led by a Black American bishop and having Black American district superintendents and others in visible leadership was a novelty for most of us. Few non-White professional persons holding positions of authority existed in our region. Though the relationships with Black American leaders were initially formal and indirect, their very presence challenged preconceived notions and images. Their presence in meetings often exposed systemic racism and contributed to the dismantling of stereotypes and racist practices.

For example, one Black American clergy leader of the newly formed Holston Area was Raymon White. Raymon was appointed as the district superintendent in Knoxville and later Johnson City. He subsequently served as president of Morristown College, a two-year college for Black American students. He was a quiet, soft-spoken man whose reserved manner has always been matched by a deep sensitivity to injustice and a willingness to courageously expose hidden prejudices and racist practices.

During a conference church extension meeting in which grant applications were being considered, a highly regarded conference lay leader presented a request on behalf of a small Black American congregation. He naïvely stated, "It's a 'colored church' but a good church." In his characteristic mellow voice, Raymon poignantly asked, "What color is it?" The room became uncomfortably silent as we felt the tension of being confronted with unconscious prejudice expressed in widely accepted language.

Two words, "colored" and "but," revealed the depth of personal and systemic racism present among us now being exposed by a simple question, "What color is it?" The embarrassed lay leader acknowledged his blunder and apologized. Raymon responded with a polite "thank you." As committee chair, I shared the embarrassment and guilt. I let the comment pass for fear of offending the lay leader. I protected my privilege, leaving it to the one most offended to make the challenge. I owed Raymon an apology, too![21]

The pervasiveness of racism raised its ugly head again in a pastors' meeting. The district superintendent announced an upcoming event at which Bishop Allen would preach. He added, "We will want to present Bishop Allen with a gift." With a chuckle, he said, "I guess we should get him a watermelon or maybe a country ham." That was 1972! One whose elevated position he owed to the bishop was blindly perpetuating demeaning racist stereotypes. Though I didn't laugh at his profane attempt at humor, I remained silent. Of the approximately fifty pastors present, only two were Black Americans. They said nothing. I wish I had at least gone to the DS privately, for it was evident from the laughter that he perpetuated and reinforced the racism among us. By my silence, I was complicit.

While integration at the higher levels of the United Methodist Church provided models of Black American

---

[21] In recognition and appreciation for Raymon's influence and contribution to my own formation, I chose him as one of the two elders to share in my consecration as a bishop in 1992.

leaders and opportunities to be together at denominational events, integration itself falls short of reconciliation and transformation of personal and societal practices. Transformative personal relationships require intentionality, vulnerability, and candid self-disclosure. Such relationships are rare, even within the church. As a colleague, in a moment of honest longing, sighed, "We seem to touch one another like marbles in a bag—on the cold, hard surface."

Relationships and Dialogue Address Prejudice and Racism

The experiences with the three congregations in Maryland illustrated the importance of dialogue and personal relationships in confronting prejudice and racism. The church's image as a center of dialogue was confirmed during my tenure as pastor of First United Methodist Church in Oak Ridge, Tennessee, in the 1980s. Oak Ridge was founded in the 1940s as a "secret city" for the purpose of developing nuclear weapons. It was a unique city composed of a high concentration of scientists, engineers, and managers of nuclear facilities. In that planned community with a highly educated population, racial and class divisions were pronounced. Housing was largely segregated along racial lines.

At a service remembering the bombing of Hiroshima and Nagasaki with bombs partially made in Oak Ridge, I met Forrest Harris, the young Black American pastor of

Oak Valley Baptist Church. We agreed to meet for lunch, which began a friendship that continues to this day. Forrest invited me to join him and his congregation in a march supporting the anti-apartheid movement in South Africa, and that led to a series of dialogues between our two congregations.

The first dialogue series centered on Martin Luther King's vision of the beloved community held on four Sunday evenings, alternating between the two churches. Forrest provided the leadership at First Church, and I led the sessions at Oak Valley. The participants spoke of how helpful the time together had been in challenging their stereotypes and prejudice. Personal friendships emerged. Exchanges followed between our choirs during worship services, and Forrest and I preached in one another's pulpit.

Similar events were held annually, and participation and relationships grew. Today, almost forty years later, a group called "The Joy Reconcilers" traces its beginning to those early experiences, a few of whom were part of those first experiences. Forrest and I joined them recently for a "reunion" and heard stories of their friendships and attendance at family weddings, funerals, and monthly gatherings.

The dialogue and exchanges between First United Methodist Church and Oak Valley Baptist Church laid the foundation for subsequent experiences as a pastor, bishop, and seminary professor. The dichotomy between the pastoral and the prophetic roles blurred in my image of ministry. Personal relationships across differences reinforced the notion that every relationship has both pastoral and prophetic dimensions. Treating everyone with respect and dignity as a beloved child of God with inherent worth and gifts AND a vision of justice, wholeness, and compassion for ALL as God's intent comprise a holistic ministry. Awareness of one's own inadequacies and participation in systemic sins contributes to a climate where dialogue is possible. The Oak Ridge experience with dialogue on race expanded to conversations on such controversial topics as nuclear weapons, genetic engineering, creationism and evolution, environmental destruction, etc.

The lessons learned as a pastor served me well as a bishop. Within the Council of Bishops in 1992, when I was elected, were Black American leaders who had become heroes. Among them were James Thomas, L. Scott Allen, Edward Carroll, who came to Oak Ridge for the dialogue on "In Defense of Creation"; W. T. Handy, who retired and lived in Nashville; Mel Talbert; Herbert Skeete; Felton May; Forrest Stith; Ernest Newmon; Woodie White; and Leontine Kelly, who participated in my consecration as bishop. Additionally, the African bishops and Black American bishops pushed the Council to confront racism within the Council, Church, and society. Their presence challenged many of the traditions and presumptuousness of the Council, and their willingness to hold privileged White Americans to account were—and continue to be—means of grace and growth in Christian discipleship.

W. T. Handy provided a particularly helpful perspective

on my own guilt and its expression. As bishop, I had to take disciplinary action against a pastor who publicly accused me of racism. I was deeply troubled by the accusation, second-guessing my decision. I made an appointment to speak with Bishop Handy, who worked at The United Methodist Publishing House. He was fully aware of the situation and knew the pastor involved. I shared my hurt and asked for Bishop Handy's response to my actions: "Please be honest with me. Are my actions in this matter fair? Am I being racist?"

"What would you have done if the pastor had been white?" the wise bishop asked.

After a few moments of introspective silence, I responded, "I would have made the same decisions, but I would have acted sooner."

"The hesitation and fear may be hints of racism, Ken," he said calmly and compassionately. Then he added, "You are widely known among the 'brothers' as someone committed to justice and racial reconciliation. And I think that is the right assessment of you, my brother."

He added something that has stayed with me over the intervening thirty years: "You are among a host of White liberals who grew up in the segregated South who genuinely want to move beyond the prejudices and racism from which you have benefitted. You likely carry unresolved guilt. The 'brothers' know that, and they will tap into that guilt, if possible, when called into account."

He assured me that my action was appropriate in

the circumstances. But he added, "It should have been done sooner." He further commented that incompetence and inappropriate behavior exist among pastors of all ethnicities and should be dealt with fairly, equitably, compassionately, firmly, and not in ways that reflect fear and unresolved guilt.

The conversation with Bishop Handy subsequently influenced how I fulfilled my oversight responsibilities in Tennessee and Mississippi. His insight transcended behaviors and incompetencies related to race. It applied to others who resisted being held accountable by appealing to their identity as evangelicals, or liberals, or women, or older, or younger. I was sensitized to be specific and candid when confronting pastors who resisted being held accountable by attempting to hook into my guilt and fears.

A New Assignment and the Move to Mississippi

Confronting racism, both personally and systemically, reached a dramatic period with my episcopal assignment to Mississippi in 2000. The initial assignment and transition created deep personal hurt, primarily due to my expectations for returning to the Nashville Area for a third quadrennium and the lack of communication and consultation with the Jurisdictional Committee on the Episcopacy.

Kern Eutsler, my former bishop, put the move in a different perspective, "Your assignment is clearly missional." A member of the episcopacy committee said, "Mississippi made a strong appeal to have you assigned. They need you!" He didn't explain the "why" of the need. Only after I arrived in Jackson did I learn that the Mississippi delegation argued the state and church needed my commitment to racial and economic justice and reconciliation. The move would have been much easier if I had been part of the conversation and told of the missional reasons.[22]

Special encouragement came from my friend Will Campbell. Will was one of four persons who escorted the Black American students who integrated the Little Rock, Arkansas, public schools in 1957 and was the only White person present for Martin Luther King, Jr.'s founding of the Southern Christian Leadership Conference. He also wrote the biography of Duncan Gray, Jr., who helped calm the angry mob when James Meredith was admitted as the first Black student at the University of Mississippi in 1962.[23] I had known Will since the 1970s when he spoke to the ministerial group in Knoxville and through our mutual involvement in visiting the prison in Nashville and advocating for criminal justice reform.

An emotional turning point occurred at the reception marking the end of my tenure as bishop of the Tennessee and Memphis Conferences. People were invited to share words of appreciation or remembrances. Will's brief comments elicited laughter from those present and encouraged me.

---

[22] It was perhaps the most emotionally intense and vocationally challenging period of my ministry. Also, shortly after our moving to Jackson, Linda's mother was diagnosed with advancing leukemia, requiring Linda's care back in Tennessee until her mother's death in June 2001. During this quadrennium, I had triple bypass surgery and two heart attacks shortly after the surgery.

[23] Will D. Campbell, *And Also with You: Duncan Gray and the American Dilemma* (Providence House Publishers, 1997).

Will tottered to the microphone with his characteristic cane looped over his arm. He said in his typical southern drawl:

Well, I'm a Baptist, and Baptists don't have much use for bishops. But Carder is the first bishop I've felt comfortable calling "bubba." Now he's going to the land of bubbas. Forty years ago, they ran me out of Mississippi. (Pause) I knew this day would come! Just consider Carder's assignment to Mississippi "Campbell's revenge!"

A local newspaper reporter unfamiliar with Will Campbell suggested that referring to me as "bubba" was "disrespectful." I countered, "On the contrary, that was the highest compliment I have received, not only tonight but during my entire ministry as a pastor and bishop!" It was Will's way of saying that I was uniquely equipped as a product of poverty and racial segregation, now with privilege and power, to be accepted in Mississippi AND to perhaps contribute to the efforts to bring reconciliation and justice where poverty and race permeated all aspects of life.

Moving into my office in Jackson, the first person to visit was Duncan Gray, Jr. He reached out his hand and said, "I'm Duncan Gray! Will Campbell sent me!" It was as though two of the early leaders in racial reconciliation in Mississippi were prodding me forward!

Indeed, the two realities central to my life and ministry came painfully to the forefront. Mississippi has been ground zero in the so-called "war on poverty" and the struggle for racial equality and justice. The state has the highest percentage of Black Americans in the U.S. (37.8 percent when I arrived in 2000) and, along with South Carolina, has the largest percentage of Black American United Methodists (approximately 17 percent in 2000). Black Americans held many key conference positions. The administrative assistant to the bishop was Reverend Joe May, who was also the leader of the delegation to General and Jurisdictional Conferences. My predecessor, Bishop Marshall (Jack) Meadors, had ensured the inclusion of Black American district superintendents to work closely with the bishop. Integration at the annual conference level had been achieved. Ethnic diversity was evident at all events, starkly contrasting my previous experience in my home conference and in the Nashville Area.

The sermon I preached at the service of welcome focused on the theme of discipleship as both being held in love and being held accountable, a topic I have often addressed since my encounter with Dr. Ferguson as a student in seminary. It included this paragraph:

> *I grew up in segregated eastern Tennessee. I didn't know any African Americans until I was an adult in seminary. Though we were poor economically, I learned early that being White meant privilege over being Black. I was formed in a world of prejudice and discrimination and was infected with the disease of racism. I have spent my life trying to overcome racism, my own and that which poisons our society. The residue of racism continues in me. If you detect prejudice and racism in me as your bishop, I invite you to confront me with it. My preference is that you come*

to me personally rather than publicly. However, I consider racism a diabolical sin, and if you need to confront me publicly, go ahead and embarrass me. I would rather lose face than lose my soul.

It was difficult for me to sense the responses. Shortly afterward, Ludwig Cameron, a Black American superintendent, said, "Bishop, do you really mean what you said, that you want to be held accountable for racism?" After assuring him that I welcome his perspective, he commented, "I appreciate your openness, but we aren't quite sure we can trust you. You must understand that you have the power to determine our future as pastors. Criticizing you personally or publicly could be costly." Then he added this needed critique, "I think you are sincere, and I want to be helpful and supportive but don't make *us* responsible for eliminating your racism. We can't take on that responsibility. That's your problem to resolve." An important lesson to learn!

The Pinnacle of Confrontation with Racism: Mississippi

An early test came within three months. Bishops William Houck of the Catholic Church, Bishop Alfred "Chip" Marble of the Episcopal Diocese of Mississippi, and Episcopal Coadjutor Bishop Duncan Gray, III, requested I join them in a public statement in support of the removal of the Confederate battle flag symbol as part of the state flag. Admittedly, I hesitated to be involved in such a volatile issue. I was new to Mississippi, an outsider. The other bishops were either native Mississippians or had lived there for decades. Having lived in Mississippi for two months, I had limited exposure among United Methodists, much less to the broader population. I knew as a general principle that building trust should precede tackling controversial issues or making significant administrative and programmatic changes.

Yet, I also knew that one does not always choose the timing when a word must be spoken. Silence would have avoided the angry responses I received from scores of White folks who chastised me for "meddling in politics," "rejecting our southern culture," "disrespecting our noble traditions," "trying to be politically correct," "creating divisions," and "failing to stick to 'spiritual' matters." A few local churches passed resolutions in support of retaining the Confederate symbol, declaring, "The bishop does not speak for us." Criticism abounded in telephone calls, letters, emails, and occasional office visits. One activist indicated my name appeared on an extremist website, and he suggested I not travel alone at night, especially in the Delta. Admittedly, the angry opposition kept me awake many nights. I became cautious when driving at night and wondered what it would all mean for my ministry in Mississippi.

Yet, support came from many sources, especially the Black American community. A statement from a Black American clergy long involved in the struggle for racial equality was especially encouraging. He expressed gratitude for the bishops making a public statement and said, "This is one of the first times White leaders have been out front. You Whites often wait until we Black folks get upset and agitated for change. But this time, a White governor and four White bishops took the lead. We are grateful!" Strong affirmations came from former Governor William Winter, veteran civil rights activists, district superintendents, and key conference leaders. The event and responses propelled me forward as an advocate for racial justice, a role applauded by the Black American community and many conference leaders AND resisted by some who considered me to be a "liberal outsider."

The efforts to change the flag failed (65 percent to 35 percent) in a referendum in April 2001. Nine years later, the Mississippi legislature approved replacing the flag, and approximately 75 percent of the voters ratified the newly designed flag. I wonder how many who opposed the efforts almost twenty years earlier were among the 75 percent.

A spirited debate early in my first annual conference session in June 2001 took on racial overtones. I don't recall the issue, only the intensity of racial divisions. When the vote was taken, only ten votes separated the winners from the losers. I quickly decided to set aside the vote, stating, "I don't think this vote accurately reflects the spirit and unity of this conference." I requested a task force be formed with an equal number of persons from both sides of the issue to see if a compromise resolution could be drafted. They were to report back the next day.

"Point of order," interrupted a delegate from the back of the auditorium. "Our standing rules state we follow *Robert's Rules of Order*, and I see no legitimate reason for you to set aside the majority vote. By what authority do you set this vote aside?" he firmly demanded.

I responded, "By the authority of 2 Corinthians 5, we have been reconciled and called to be agents of reconciliation. If the task force cannot reach a compromise resolution to bring before the conference or the conference does not approve the new resolution, then the vote will stand. I am asking that we attempt to live the reconciliation that has already been wrought in Jesus Christ."

The following day, the task force presented a resolution that was approved almost unanimously. Although my action was outside the standing rules, it was important to establish an authority beyond *Robert's Rules* and to make clear that my priority was reconciliation. The action enhanced credibility among Black American leaders and others committed to finding ways to bridge the racial divide.

Journeys of Remembrance, Repentance, and Reconciliation

During the 2000-2004 quadrennium, I served as president of the General Board of Discipleship. An initiative on the agenda was the printing of the *Upper Room Devotional* magazine in Africa. Present at one of the board meetings was Ross Olivier,[24] the General Secretary of the Methodist Church of Southern Africa. We immediately connected on a personal level, and a friendship developed. Emerging from our conversations was the idea of conducting a series of "journeys of remembrance, repentance, and reconciliation," patterned loosely after an initiative in South Africa and the Truth and Reconciliation Commission.

The cabinet enthusiastically supported the idea and began meeting in communities where key events occurred in the civil rights struggles. Charles Marsh's *God's Long Summer,* which chronicles the events and personalities involved in the critical summer of 1964, provided the background.[25] People involved in the event were invited to participate and share their experiences. The format included sharing memories, feelings associated with those memories, the impact of those events, and what we learned from them. Ed King, a clergy member of the conference and a leading participant in the protests of 1964, accompanied us on the journeys. Two of those gatherings are particularly memorable.

The first journey was to Neshoba County, near Philadelphia, Mississippi, and Mt. Zion United Methodist Church. The church had been a center of activism on behalf of voting rights and was burned in 1964. On June

---

[24] In 2004, I appointed Ross Olivier as senior pastor of Galloway Memorial United Methodist Church in Jackson, which on Easter Sunday, 1964, had turned away Bishop Charles Golden and Bishop James Matthews from attending worship.

[25] Charles Marsh, *God's Long Summer: Stories of Faith and Civil Rights* (Princeton University Press, 1997).

21, 1964, activists James Chaney, Andrew Goodman, and Michael Schwerner came to investigate the burning of the church. Leaving the church, they were arrested and subsequently murdered by the KKK, which included state and county law enforcement officers.

Members of the Mt. Zion congregation were invited to be part of the conversation, along with retired Bishop Clay Lee, the pastor of Philadelphia's First Methodist Church in 1964. Ed King shared a recording of the funeral for James Chaney at which he spoke. Among the participants was Mrs. Steele, a member of Mt. Zion. Now elderly and in a wheelchair, with great emotion, she shared memories of the events surrounding the murders. Fighting back tears, she said softly, "I remember it as though it was yesterday. I don't know why they killed them. They were such nice young men." Ed King and Clay Lee shared their recollections of the aftermath of the meeting on June 21, 1964.

Bishop Lee had been my bishop in Holston Conference. I knew that he, like many of us White American clergy, harbored ambivalent feelings about our level of involvement in the 1960s. While we may have spoken out occasionally and participated in efforts for justice, most of us did so from a safe distance. Compared to Ed King, who bore a facial scar from the violence of that era, we did little. Lee had served as an associate pastor at churches that turned away Black Americans from attending worship during integration efforts in 1963 and 1964. Had he been too complicit with segregation and taken the easy way out?[26] I knew he had raised that question of himself. He shared with the group how he came to Mt. Zion Church after it was burned to pledge help from First Church. He received threatening phone calls, and many in his congregation opposed his reaching out.

Ed King then recounted his efforts on behalf of integration and voting rights. He was a native of Mississippi and a graduate of Boston University School of Theology. He served as a leader of the Freedom Summer and worked closely with Chaney, Goodman, and Schwerner. Following Ed's presentation, a district superintendent asked to comment.

"I want to apologize to you, Ed. As you recall, we were candidates for ordination and membership in the annual conference the same year. I was admitted, but you were not.[27] I knew what was happening was wrong, but I said nothing. I'm sorry, and I ask for your forgiveness."

Ed responded, "Yes, I forgive you! We all had our blind spots then. The important question is, what are our blind spots now? Where are we remaining silent and passive when we should be speaking and acting?"

---

[26] During a conversation with Will Campbell many years later, he said, "I used to think that Clay Lee sold out, that he compromised too much. But I realize all of us Whites compromised. I compromised by moving out of Mississippi while he stayed. Maybe he did more to bring change by compromising and staying than I did by leaving."

[27] Ed had graduated from Boston School of Theology and was eligible for admission to the conference as what is now called a "provisional member." At the time of the annual conference session, he had been arrested for a sit-in demonstration in Jackson and jailed. He was released from jail to attend the session and was denied admission.

A middle-aged Black American man, who had arrived after Clay Lee had spoken, interrupted: "It isn't just White folks who have blind spots. Black people do, too. And some speak up, and others don't, in both races." After a moment's pause, he continued, "There was a pastor at First Methodist Church ..." I became anxious. I looked at Clay Lee and his wife and saw the tenseness on their faces. What is he going to say? Is he going to embarrass Clay by suggesting that he missed his opportunity?

He continued, "He spoke out. He said, 'It's wrong to shed innocent blood, and those young men who were murdered were innocent.' I don't remember his name or what happened to him, but he didn't stay silent."

Looking toward Clay, I asked the one who had interrupted, "Would you like to meet that pastor? He's here on the second row." Suddenly, tension fell away, and tears filled the eyes of many, including the Lees. A spirit of forgiveness, affirmation, and hope arrived and pervaded the remainder of the gathering.

Clay Lee indicated to me later when he was president of the local ministerial association in 1964, the group drafted a statement that included, "It's wrong to shed innocent blood, and those young men were innocent." He had delivered the statement over the radio, and it was printed in the newspaper. The man who had just spoken was Mrs. Steele's son. Only eleven at the time, he and his mother were at the church the night it was burned. Who would have dreamed that a simple statement by a ministerial association would influence a young child whose memory of it would be a means of healing and reconciliation forty years later?

A service of remembrance marking the fortieth anniversary of Freedom Summer was held in June 2004 at Mt. Zion Church. The small rural church was filled with diverse people from across the nation. Veteran activists from the 1960s were among the crowd, now in their waning years. Clay Lee and I were invited to participate in remembering James Chaney, Andrew Goodman, and Michael Schwerner. What a sobering and profound honor it was for me to light the candle in memory of James Chaney. Following the memorial service, we boarded buses for the short trip to the auditorium in Philadelphia, Mississippi, where Congressman John Lewis challenged the large crowd to remember that justice and reconciliation require we learn from the past and build for the future.

Another journey took us to Ruleville in the Mississippi Delta, the home of Fanny Lou Hamer. In preparation, participants read about Ms. Hamer's life and work in *God's Long Summer*. She helped to organize Mississippi Freedom Summer and was active in the Student Non-Violent Coordinating Committee and Southern Christian Leadership Conference. She served as vice-chair of the Freedom Democratic Party and participated in the protest at the 1964 National Democratic Party Convention. Her efforts resulted in the registration of thousands of Black Americans to vote. Violence at the hands of police, the KKK, and society's injustice accompanied her until death in 1974 at the age of fifty-seven.

Our journey began that morning working alongside members of the Ruleville community in painting a Habitat house. We gathered for lunch at the United Methodist Church with those who had known Ms. Hamer. We sat around the table as people shared stories of experiences with Ms. Hamer and expressions of gratitude for her life and witness. We heard accounts of her beatings and cruelty at the hands of authorities and other racists.

Fred Brown, one of the superintendents, confessed that this was the first time he had felt comfortable expressing in a group of White folks that Ms. Hamer was "my hero." Another Black American leader nodded in agreement. Then, a White American superintendent said, "I'm sorry, Fred. I once considered her a 'troublemaker.' But I want you to know she is now my hero, too!"

Following lunch, we gathered around Ms. Hamer's grave. Etched on her tombstone is one of her most famous quotes: "I'm sick and tired of being sick and tired." We shared reflections and feelings, ranging from guilt to gratitude, regret to recommitment. Joining hands, we sang her favorite song, "This little light of mine, I'm going to let it shine," followed by the doxology. Tears and laughter mingled as Black and White Americans embraced. Fanny Lou Hamer's hope for change became a reality, at least among those few gathered at her resting place.

Other journeys took us to Holly Springs and Rust College, Brookhaven and McComb, Gulfside Assembly, and Jackson State University. We listened to stories of pain, violence, discrimination, regret, guilt, and loss AND stories of resilience, courage, compassion, and hope. People who lived the same heritage but played different roles came together in vulnerability, repentance, reconciliation, and a yearning for the beloved community.

During these gatherings, painful memories surfaced of my inadequate responses to the injustice of racism, playing it safe when I should have spoken out, or remaining in my secure spaces when presence with those on the frontlines was needed. A woman in McComb brought my feelings to the forefront. She told her story of discrimination and abuse by privileged White folks. She added, "This is the first time I've felt safe telling my story to a group of White people."

She then looked toward me and said, "Thank you! I wish you had been the bishop back then. Things would have been different."

I confessed, "I like to think that I would have been present with you, listened to your pain, and helped to overcome the injustices you and your family were experiencing. But I'm not sure I would have been different from the bishop who was here at the time. I could have done more then. I had my blind spots, my prejudices, my failures. You have helped me face those by telling your story, and you have made me want to do more. Thank you!"

The value of the journeys was summarized twenty years later by one of the participants. He affirmed the emphasis on racial justice and reconciliation as having "opened my eyes to the truth of the evil present in our state. Our trip to the exhibit at Jackson State (of lynchings) helped me get a full view of that evil. Our journeys to sites around the state where we heard survivor testimonies were like peeling an onion one layer at a time, revealing how pervasive the evil was and, in many ways, still is."

The Struggle Continues

Race continues as America's "original sin," though the overt manifestations have changed. As the aphorism declares, "History doesn't repeat itself, but it does often rhyme." Present conditions mirror our country's ugly history of division, prejudice, exploitation, and injustice rooted in race. Politicians popularly exploit unresolved racial tensions, and discussions of systemic, institutionalized racism are politicized as "woke." Though services of repentance for racism have been conducted and volumes have been written about slavery's deadly infection of American culture, racism continues to dominate our economic, political, social, and religious practices and policies. Our ritualized repentance has not resulted in bringing forth "fruits worthy of repentance" (Matthew 3:8).

My world remains largely segregated. I'm surrounded by privileged White neighbors. I participate in a local church with only White Americans. My grandkids went to public schools with few non-white students and teachers. The professionals from whom I receive services—doctors, lawyers, accountants, bankers, managers, editors, pastors—are White. Yet, the people who cleaned my house, mowed the grass, cooked, and served the food in the retirement community where I lived for ten years are mostly non-White. Most who bathe, feed, and tend to the frail in the nursing facilities there are Black Americans. The historic power dynamics remain intact.

The same was true during my years working in academia. Most tenured faculty and administrators were White Americans, and the ethos of White elitism prevailed in the policies, curriculum, and pedagogy. Subtle and sometimes blatant forms of racial prejudice seeped through the veneer of scholarly sophistication and polished administrative leadership. Candid conversations with housekeeping staff, student advisees, and minority faculty members revealed much underlying pain from intimidation, insensitivity, and blindness to power differentials and unacknowledged structures of White privilege.

Institutionalized policies and practices operate as invisible forces of segregation, discrimination, exploitation, and even violence. My South African friend Peter Storey was prominently involved in the anti-apartheid struggle, working closely with Desmond Tutu for many years. Peter says that when institutions and systems do our sinning for us, it's easier to claim innocence and deny personal responsibility. Our privilege isolates us from the adverse consequences of those institutionalized policies on those without privilege. For example, an educational system that suggests slavery was beneficial to enslaved people literally "whitewashes" exploitation of Black Americans. Or a criminal justice system with racist underpinning and practices reinforces negative stereotypes and helps us rationalize our fears. A housing system that segregates people into homogeneous neighborhoods makes personal relationships across racial and economic lines difficult, thereby enabling us to avoid the pain and suffering of those different from ourselves.

My wife, Linda, required extensive medical care for the last ten years of her life. Four of those years, she required around-the-clock care. With a few exceptions, her closest care companions were Black American women. Although they worked for an agency that determined their wages and schedules, they became our friends and confidants. These women performed the most basic and intimate tasks for a privileged White American couple. I admittedly felt like a plantation owner with Black American servants doing the dirty work. They were paid a little above minimum wage with no pension or health insurance. That's the system! My familiar guilt surfaced.

After several weeks, I opened up with the care providers, all of whom were members of one family. We had learned much about one another and our families. They knew my background growing up, and they were aware of the various positions I had held. I knew much about their stories. They had experienced my vulnerability and tears as Linda declined, and I felt increasingly comfortable in sharing feelings with them.

Here is the essence of what I told each of them:

I really appreciate your sensitive care of Linda, and I want to always treat you fairly and respectfully. I know you work for [Name of Agency], but you are more than needed workers in my house. I consider you friends and colleagues in Linda's care. However, I am conscious that you are Black, and I am White. I can't imagine how it feels to be doing menial, intimate tasks for White folks, given the history of this country. I never want to treat you as less than a person of inherent worth and dignity. If you ever feel that I am treating you as less, please tell me.

Trust between us strengthened. I heard stories of their ongoing experiences of racial discrimination and abuse. Being stopped for "driving while Black" has been experienced by all driving members of their family. Subjection to verbal insults and demeaning actions from patients and their families was accepted as "part of the job." Sexual overtures and harassment are no strangers to them. They struggle to pay bills, and a car breakdown is a major economic crisis.

While personal compassion, empathy, and respect are foundational, they must be translated into concrete actions to dismantle racism and change the political, economic, and healthcare systems that operate as echoes of slavery. How I use the power of my privilege to change the systems remains at the forefront of my current struggle! It is made more challenging by the current climate of political polarization and dysfunction, the normalization of hatred, bigotry, and disrespect of "the other," and the church's preoccupation with institutional survival.

Yet, we do not lose heart. Hope abounds! Signs of crumbling barriers exist for those with eyes to see. For disciples of Jesus, the decisive sign lies in the declaration of the Apostle Paul:

All this is from God, who reconciled us to himself through Christ, and has given us the ministry of reconciliation; that is, in Christ God was reconciling the world unto himself, not counting their trespasses against them, and entrusting the message of reconciliation to us.

2 Corinthians 5:18-19

Conclusion

A poster with a quote from James Baldwin hung in my office for years: "Not everything that is faced can be changed; but nothing can be changed until it is faced."[28] Honestly confronting racism and White privilege is a process and runs counter to prevailing structures and practices in American society. Denial and avoidance are built into the systems in which we live. My journey *toward* has been lifelong and remains a deep yearning. Here are some of the truths I continue to face in the pursuit of "the beloved community":

- Racism and White privilege are pervasive and endemic in American society, and I am guilty and accountable for my own participation in them.
- Confronting my guilt and participation is an essential component of healing and reconciliation.

---

[28] *The New York Times*, January 14, 1962.

- I need diverse personal relationships in community to expose my blind spots.

- Confession and vulnerability provide an atmosphere of trust and honesty.

- Change in attitudes, behaviors, and systems begins with personal relationships across racial barriers.

- While I need community and persons of other races to overcome my racism and prejudices, they are not responsible for eradicating my racism.

- Empathetically hearing the stories and experiences of others facilitates understanding and reconciliation.

- Dialogue across racial barriers in an atmosphere of mutual respect is an effective means of dismantling racism and fostering reconciliation.

- The church is uniquely positioned to be a center of dialogue and reconciliation.

- Integration only provides the *opportunity* for effecting justice and reconciliation.

- Although overt expressions of racial prejudice may have changed, the underlying systems and attitudes mirror our history of slavery and bigotry.

- Changing systems represents the most formidable challenge confronting us and requires more than personal empathy and compassion.

- Hope lies in the assurance that our efforts on behalf of justice and reconciliation are a participation in God's mission as experienced in Jesus the Christ.

CHAPTER SEVEN

"I Was in Prison ..."

A Judge's Challenge

A speech by federal judge Frank Wilson at the 1966 annual conference significantly shaped my life and ministry. Judge Wilson shared that he kept in contact with every person he sentenced to prison. His rationale for writing or visiting inmates was simple: he didn't want his only impact on an individual to be the act of denying their freedom.

This highly regarded jurist added, "Pastors should be as familiar with the inside of the local jails and prisons as they are the local hospitals." As a young pastor, I had visited hospitals almost daily, but I had never been inside a jail. Within a few weeks of the judge's challenge, I made my first visit to the county jail. I reluctantly, anxiously entered a world often hidden from and ignored by congregations and pastors. There, I met more than law enforcement officers and inmates. I met the One who said, "I was in prison, and you visited me."

Entering a New World … Behind the Bars

The prospect of visiting the jail scared me. Law enforcement folks intimidated me. Relating to inmates seemed daunting. Prison ministry wasn't in the seminary curriculum, and my clinical pastoral training was in a hospital. I knew little about the criminal justice system. Still, Judge Wilson's admonition felt like a divine mandate.

My first visit was with the sheriff, who was rightly suspicious of this naïve pastor. I told him of Judge Wilson's challenge and my openness to learn from the sheriff's experience. He indicated that the men in the jail "don't like to be preached to." He further cautioned against being manipulated by the prisoners. "If you will go to the judge on their behalf and get them off, you'll be popular, but that's not what they need from you." He explained the visitation rules. My visits would be in cell blocks with bars between me and the men. If someone requested a private visit, the jailer would lock me and that person in a separate holding cell for the visit.

Trust developed over the next few weeks as I got acquainted with jail staff, including the chief deputy and jailer. I learned quickly that the men in the cells did not like "that preacher that yells at us every week over the intercom." Much of the conversation with me was guarded since there was little privacy. I learned their names and often asked simply, "How are things going?"

During one of my visits, a young man asked to speak privately. Ed was a muscular man whose arms were covered with tattoos. "Born to Lose" was inscribed on his left arm, and "Born to Raise Hell" on his right. He immediately blurted out, "How do I get God in my life?"

"Why," I asked, "do you want God in your life? What difference do you think that will make?"

For the next several minutes, he shared a story of abuse, foster homes, and repeated incarcerations. Sorrowfully, he added, "I've made a mess of my life. I want to amount to something. I've hurt a lot of people, and I ain't worth nothin'."

I responded, "Ed, you don't have to *get* God in your life. God is already present *in* you. Your guilt and regret, the longing to make something of your life, the desire for a sense of worth—that *is* God's presence with you. We can begin by thanking God for being present in those feelings and desires and then open your whole life to that Presence."

What theologians call "prevenient grace" took on a new meaning in that conversation. We never *take* God anywhere; we *find* God already present.

Ed helped me learn that the Christian gospel must be more than a theological abstraction; it must be embodied. How was Ed to know the meaning of love when all he had known was rejection? How could he understand forgiveness when vengeance and retribution had dominated his experience? How was he to experience worth and dignity rooted in grace when society's treatment reinforced his feelings of worthlessness?

The men behind the bars weren't the only ones who

impacted me. Those who arrested and locked them up became friends and means of grace. One was the chief deputy. He was widely known in the community for making arrests and often appeared in the news. His image was one of no-nonsense toughness.

One evening, the news reported that a man had been killed by an officer responding to a domestic abuse call. The chief deputy had been wounded in the altercation. Upon request, I visited the deputy in the intensive care unit at the hospital. Over the next several visits, he shared feelings of deep sadness, regret, and guilt. Haunting questions dominated the conversations: What could I have done differently? Did I enter the house too abruptly? Could I have negotiated with him? How is his wife doing? Does she blame me? Do they have children? Talk of grief, forgiveness, and reconciliation was often through tears and sighs too deep for words.

As the deputy prepared to leave the hospital, he asked if I would arrange a visit with the widow. Though hesitant and insecure, I made a call to the home where the shooting occurred. After introducing myself as a pastor and a volunteer chaplain at the jail, she welcomed me inside. I expressed regret for the tragedy and told her I had come at the deputy's request. Through tears, she unleashed her own sadness, regret, and guilt—the same feelings expressed by the deputy. She agreed to the visit.

Still weak from his serious wounds, the deputy and I visited the woman. For more than an hour, I listened to their confessions of profound regret and sensed their yearning for forgiveness and reconciliation. She apologized for putting the deputy in the situation with her call, and he countered with his regret for taking her husband's life. I simply listened, occasionally reflecting to them the feelings they were verbalizing. As we ended our visit, we prayed together, and I left feeling I had been on holy ground.

During a subsequent visit at the jail, an emergency call came that a mentally disturbed man was "acting out," and law enforcement was needed. The chief deputy knew the history of violence with Cedrick (not his real name), including violence toward police. He asked that I accompany him to the home.

As we approached the home in an unmarked car, the deputy shared that Cedrick had played college football and was exceptionally strong. Previous attempts to subdue him resulted in injuries. The sight of uniformed, armed police would likely trigger his anger and physical resistance. The deputy radioed ahead that all police officers were to remain out of view and would be called in only if necessary.

Cedrick's mother, who had made the 9-1-1 call, opened the door and invited us in. The large, muscular young man was pacing back and forth, agitated and hostile. Hallucinations were part of his mental illness, and imaginary people were threatening him. For several minutes, we tried to interrupt his anguish with words of assurance. The deputy spoke softly to him about football and how we wanted to help him. I introduced myself as a pastor there to support him and his mother. Cedrick's conversation veered off into an incoherent discussion of some mathematical formula. We patiently listened and tried to calm him for several minutes, only to see him become increasingly agitated and physically active. I frankly got scared that he would erupt into violence.

The deputy left the room to make a call. He arranged for a sedative to be brought to the house. He returned to the room where I had unsuccessfully attempted to bring calm, though he had stopped pacing. The deputy carried three glasses of grape juice and announced it was time for refreshments. He had mixed the medication in the glass given to Cedrick, who calmly drank the juice. Gradually, the mood changed; the voice grew calm, and he grew quiet.

The deputy said, "Cedrick, we need to go for a ride. We want to take you to a place where they can make you better. Come on, we'll go with you." He stood up. We got on each side of him. We took hold of his gigantic arms and walked toward the waiting unmarked police car. We placed him in the back seat, where he quickly fell asleep on the way to the hospital.

I suspect that had this incident occurred before the deputy's deadly encounter with violence a few months earlier, a different outcome would have resulted. This time, the priority response was an alternative to violent force. A tough cop was foremost a human being who shared the same feelings, yearnings, and needs as those he arrested.

Relationships, Networking, and Support

Personal relationships with incarcerated persons, their families, and law enforcement officials shaped my reading and continuing education activities. I learned the difference between *retributive justice* based on punishment and *restorative justice*, which seeks reconciliation and restoration of community. While the American system may give occasional lip service to rehabilitation and "correction," retribution dominates the practice. "Lock them up" is a prevailing response to crime. The United States, with five percent of the world's population, houses twenty-five percent of the world's prison population. Furthermore, the U.S. has one of the highest recidivism rates in the world, indicating that incarceration does not work as a solution to crime.

Persons in jails and prisons are predominantly economically poor. Many have a history of mental illness. Drug and alcohol addiction and physical and emotional abuse are familiar stories. A disproportionate number of them are ethnic minorities and poor and bear the marks of racial discrimination and injustice. Prisons and jails portray in microcosm the complex systemic challenges in our society: economic disparity and poverty, drug and alcohol abuse, racism and prejudice, family breakdown and dysfunction, inadequate educational system, isolation and loneliness, and political/governmental failure.

Behind the walls of every prison and jail are fathers and mothers, sons and daughters, husbands and wives, friends and neighbors. All are persons made in the divine image who, like the rest of us, have distorted that image but long for love, reconciliation, hope, and purpose. I realized early that ministry among those living behind prison walls requires more than personal one-on-one visitation, as important as such presence is.

While living in Abingdon, Virginia, I became involved in efforts to provide a more holistic approach. Offender Aid and Restoration (OAR) attempted to shift the focus from punishment to rehabilitation. Volunteers from local congregations were trained and supervised to work with deemed "offenders" and their families in addressing their individual challenges. Initiating the program required the cooperation of the county sheriff and other governmental officials. Funding had to be secured and leadership identified and employed. Through ecumenical involvement, political advocacy, and numerous one-on-one negotiations, the program was implemented.

Specific programs emerged in response to identified needs. Recruiting and training volunteers to become friends with those confined in the jail was a priority. Tutoring, job training, counseling, educational opportunities through the local community college, and addiction treatment emerged among the organized activities.

The OAR program laid the foundation to engage lay people in congregations with the criminal justice system and its challenges and opportunities. Those efforts included educational experiences led by those with knowledge and experience. One approach was partnering with existing ministries such as Kairos, Yokefellows, and Prison Fellowship. Always, the key was fostering relationships.

Prisons isolate people from their families and support systems. Many are incarcerated in remote or faraway facilities, and their families lack means of transportation to visit them. Concord United Methodist Church initiated a bus ministry by using the church van and volunteer drivers to transport family members to the state prison once each month. Not only were families connected with their loved ones, but the volunteer drivers also developed friendships, provided support, and learned from the people they transported.

While driving on a backroad near Concord Church on a cold November afternoon, I noticed smoke from the chimney of a shanty on the hillside. Although I had passed that way previously, I assumed no one lived in the small, rundown house. I parked and walked across the field to the house, where I found a young pregnant mother with a toddler son huddled around the wood stove. I introduced myself as the pastor of the United Methodist Church nearby and expressed that I simply wanted to meet them.

Katie (not her real name) indicated she had just moved in and didn't know anyone. She then shared that her husband was in prison in Nashville, leaving her alone to care for their son. It was evident she needed assistance. But how do I offer help while preserving her dignity and self-respect? I asked if it would be okay if I arranged to get her some groceries. She readily agreed.

A women's circle and a Sunday School class expressed interest in connecting with a family in need for Thanksgiving and Christmas. We established that such a connection would be entered only with the understanding that the relationship would be long-term. Based on my own childhood experience, I resist treating people as projects or objects of charity, which can rob them of their dignity. However, the impulse to help those in need can be a springboard for developing long-term friendships with people living on the margins, and from those relationships, awareness of systemic realities and commitment to justice and charity may emerge.

A couple of women from the church volunteered to deliver groceries and be the primary contacts with Katie. As trust developed, others were invited into the circle of care. One was a doctor who enabled her to get prenatal care. After several weeks, the women threw her a "baby shower" at the church. What a sign of the kingdom! Wrapped items needed for a newborn were piled high. Laughter filled the room and hallway. Through tears of joy and gratitude, Kate was overheard saying, "I ain't never had a party before!" Hers weren't the only tears.

As months passed and the baby was born, the relationships continued. With encouragement and assistance, Katie was connected to public assistance resources, including housing. She successfully developed new relationships, and accessed additional resources. She became more self-confident and independent. She entered a job training program and earned her GED.

Regrettably, Katie's husband lacked the same attention in prison. Attempts to connect with him were unsuccessful. The supportive community surrounding Katie was missing for him. Upon release, he returned to a different Katie. There was no community welcoming him home and providing resources such as job training, counseling, and encouragement. Their marriage collapsed. He became one of the many parolees who return to prison within months of being released.

Tension: Presence Versus Public Advocacy and Political Engagement

Public criticism of the local jail's conditions resulted in our denied permission to visit. Dr. L. Harold DeWolf, a well-known theologian who taught at Boston School of Theology and was the major advisor in Dr. Martin Luther King's Th.D. dissertation, led a conference at the church I served in the Knoxville area. I shared the experience of being prevented from visiting the local jail, and he advised that, in some situations, pastors must make compromises between public advocacy and one-on-one relationships with persons behind bars. Paid prison chaplains persistently live with the tension between prophetic advocacy and pastoral presence. Dr. DeWolf cautioned that I avoid seeing one as superior to the other. Both advocacy and personal relationships are important components of prison ministry.

Advocacy on behalf of criminal justice reform is enhanced when we can speak out of personal engagements. During testimony before a Mississippi legislative committee considering a moratorium on state executions, a legislator asked, "But what about concern for the victims?" I responded that concern for victims lies at the core of my opposition to the death penalty. I then shared the story of my relationship with a mother whose mentally challenged son was executed.

The son was incarcerated in another state, and the mother kept secret her son's fate. Upon visiting with the mother, I learned she was an active member of a local United Methodist Church. Neither the pastor nor church friends knew of her situation. I talked with her by phone ten minutes after she received word of her son's execution. This mother loved her son no less than the mother of her son's victims. I listened to her wailing, her isolation, her anguish. The state that executed her son created additional victims.

A Governor's Manipulation of Justice

In an interview with a news reporter, Tennessee Governor Ray Blanton indicated he intended to pardon a convicted murderer named Roger Humphreys. Humphreys, the son of a political ally of the governor, had been convicted of second-degree murder for killing his ex-wife and her boyfriend. A firestorm of protests erupted. In response, the governor promised to have the commissioner of the Department of Corrections appoint a "Blue Ribbon Committee" to evaluate Humphreys' eligibility for a pardon.

I was shocked to receive an invitation from the commissioner to be part of the committee. I was very hesitant for several reasons. One, I didn't want to get involved in a highly controversial public political conflict. Further, I felt unqualified and was busy pastoring an active, growing congregation.[29]

I told the commissioner I did not want to be embroiled in a partisan political ploy to solve the governor's public relations problem. The commissioner assured me the committee was nonpartisan and would be unrestricted in exploring the facts and its recommendations. When asked if Governor Blanton would abide by the committee's recommendation, he assured me the governor had so promised.

After consulting with Bishop Finger and the chair of the staff-parish relations committee, I agreed to serve. Among the committee members were a forensic psychiatrist, prison chaplain, Republican state senator, Democratic state representative, newspaper publisher, criminal defense lawyer, prosecutor, former member of the parole board, and professor of criminal law at Vanderbilt.

After months of public meetings, testimony from key witnesses, and information gathering, the governor asked

---

[29] After agreeing to serve, I learned that the man killed was the son of Dr. Kenneth Scholl, the doctor who delivered me and after whom I was named. I offered to resign but was persuaded to remain.

to meet with us in a closed session. Having agreed that all meetings would be open, we declined the invitation. The governor rejected the opportunity to share input in a public session and thereafter attempted to discredit the committee. I shared reasons for opposing Mr. Humphreys' pardon in our final meeting. I indicated I have great empathy for those serving time in prison and feel that incarceration is not the solution to crime. However, justice requires fairness and equity of treatment, and the guidelines for pardon and parole should be applied equitably based on the agreed-upon criteria, not upon political patronage and favoritism. Mr. Humphreys clearly did not meet the guidelines.

Though the committee voted unanimously against granting the pardon, the governor ignored the recommendation and freed Mr. Humphreys and others. Governor Blanton was later convicted of fraud and sentenced to prison. Some of his staff members were convicted of various crimes, including selling pardons.

The Humphreys case illustrates the multi-faceted realities and conflicts within the criminal justice system. The vision of the blindfolded lady balancing the scales of justice remains unfulfilled, and conflicting goals prevail. Crime becomes a central issue during election cycles, but critical thinking related to the criminal justice system is left to a few academics and activists. Politicians use crime as a fear tactic and, thereby, add to the ineffectiveness of the criminal justice system and the stigmatization of those who live in prisons and jails. Left unaddressed are the systemic problems of racism and economic disparities underlying the current system.

A Friend on Death Row: The Ultimate Absurdity and Failure of the System

A statement attributed to Fyodor Dostoevsky declares, "The degree of civilization in a society can be judged by entering its prisons."[30] Indeed, prisons and death chambers expose the barbarism within the United States. Approximately twenty-four hundred people currently live on death row in the U.S. Though the number has declined in recent years, calls for more executions continue. No evidence exists that the death penalty serves as a deterrent or "brings closure" to the victims of murder. It only adds to the culture of violence and avoids coming to grips with our society's failures.

My daughter, Sheri, initiated my first visit to death row. As the editor of her high school newspaper, she sought to write an article on the death penalty, and she wanted to interview someone on death row. After several weeks of navigating the bureaucratic maze of the Tennessee State Corrections system, Sheri and I were cleared to visit William (Bill) Groseclose. Bill's trustworthiness as a prisoner and the ease with which he interacted with inmates, correction officers, and visitors made him a "safe" interviewee.

---

[30] Verification of the quote is disputed as described in https://lareviewofbooks.org/article/dostoyevsky-misprisioned-the-house-of-the-dead-and-american-prison-literature/.

In October 1982, Sheri and I drove from Knoxville to Nashville for our first visit with Bill. I tried to prepare my sixteen-year-old daughter to enter the bleak, dangerous, and insecure world behind prison bars, but I wasn't quite prepared for the scene we were about to enter.

The Tennessee State Penitentiary that housed the death unit was one of the worst in the nation. A federal lawsuit had been filed charging that the prison's conditions amounted to "cruel and unusual punishment." The state was under court order to improve the conditions at the old fortress-like facility that had opened in 1898.[31] Behind the high stone walls with towers sheltering heavily armed guards lived two thousand men, almost double the facility's capacity.

After receiving passes and undergoing pat-down searches, Sheri and I made our way through six iron gates before reaching the interior prison yard. Men in prison uniforms roamed the area, some huddled in small groups, others sitting idly against the fortressed walls. Lining the yard were stone buildings housing inmates who were not permitted to mingle with the general prison population.

As we walked through the prison yard toward the concrete building called Unit Six, we felt the stares of curious inmates and the watchful eyes of heavily armed guards. "Cat calls" and whistles came from the barred windows of the adjacent cells as our red-haired daughter and I made our way to "death row."

---

[31] Scenes in the movie *The Green Mile* were filmed inside the facility a few years after it closed in 1985.

Entering the fortified door into Unit Six, Sheri and I immediately saw one of the nation's most infamous inmates, James Earl Ray, mopping the floor in the entranceway. We were escorted into a dimly lit, concrete-walled room with no windows. The furnishings comprised a steel table anchored to the floor, six chairs, and a wall-mounted blackboard. The door locked behind us. This was the visitation room for those permitted to have face-to-face visits. It doubled as the classroom for death row inmates permitted to participate in limited educational activities. As Sheri and I waited nervously for Bill to be escorted into the room, we noticed a hand-drawn image of Jesus on the chalkboard. Underneath the drawing, it said: "Jesus, our brother, lives on death row."

The door opened, and a handcuffed-but-smiling Bill was escorted into the room. He greeted us with a joyful "Hello! You must be Sheri and Reverend Carder." He presented Sheri with his painting of a Smurf with pen and paper in hand, representing a journalist. The officer removed his cuffs. We warmly shook hands and took our seats around the table. The officer moved to one side but remained nearby, listening and observing throughout the visit.

Bill had introduced himself in a series of letters before our visit. Born in 1948 in southwestern Virginia, he was the father of four children. He had been in the Navy and was serving as a recruiter when, in 1977, he was charged with having his wife killed. He was convicted and sentenced to death in 1978. Although we did not discuss his case, Bill claimed innocence and was appealing his conviction.

During our two-hour visit, Bill shared about his family background, his daily life on death row, his views on the death penalty, and more. The conversation was mixed with levity and serious reflections. Bill was exceptionally smart, articulate, well-read, and informed on multiple current and historical issues. He described the conditions under which he and his fellow inmates lived, including daily exposure to rats and roaches, suffocating heat in summer, and chilling cold in winter. He talked freely about his potential walk to the death chamber at the end of his hallway that housed "Ole Smokey," the name given to the electric chair.

I asked, "Bill, given the circumstances under which you live, how do you maintain hope and a sense of humor?" He responded, "The philosophers got it right. Some things in life are so tragic that you cry. Others are so comical that the only appropriate response is laughter. But most things are a mixture of tragedy and comedy. In those, you have a choice. You can choose to laugh or cry. When I have the choice, I choose to laugh." Pointing to the drawing of Jesus on the chalkboard (which we learned he had drawn), he added, "That helps, too. We aren't alone here."

What began as a high school newspaper project resulted in a transforming friendship that spanned decades. Frequent letters, regular telephone calls, and occasional visits followed our initial visit. Bill's letters to Sheri were filled with advice and encouragement as she graduated from high school and college, married, and became a mother. We assumed responsibility for managing the meager finances earned from his prison work. We were the beneficiaries of his artistic and craft talents as they now decorate our homes.

Multiple appeals were filed and dismissed. Execution dates were set and postponed over twenty years. On one occasion, Bill came within three days of being executed. Living conditions improved, partly as a result of the petition Bill filed in federal court on behalf of his friends on death row. The federal judge, who made an unannounced visit to the old fortress prison Unit Six, ruled in favor of the petition, resulting in the building of a new prison.

Bill's behavior and skills earned him a "trustee" status, and he was assigned to work in the unit supervisor's office. He taught GED classes, painting, and Bible classes to fellow inmates in the unit, and he continued his learning by taking college-level correspondence courses on various subjects, including the Bible and theology.

Times with Bill included the comedic and the tragic, laughter and tears. Neither title nor position mattered to him. He never called me "Reverend" after our introductory visit. I was always "Ken" or "my friend." His guilt or innocence was not a judgment I needed to make. He was always able to detect pretense and seemed to have intuitive empathy. If he detected posturing in me or others, he would laughingly dismantle it, saying, "Now, you can't con a con!"

Our friendship reached a turning point in 1992 when I was elected to the episcopacy. The afternoon of my election, a call came to our house at Lake Junaluska. Upon answering the phone, Linda called to me, "It's Bill!" "Bill who?" I asked. "Bill Groseclose," she responded, almost in tears. I went to the phone, and the first words I heard were, "Finally, an American election that turns out right."

"How did you know? How are you making this call?" I asked, realizing that calls from inmates are monitored and costly. He indicated that the associate pastor had called the prison to get word to him, and he happened to be working in the office at the time. "But who gave you permission to call?" I inquired. "That's another story, and I'll tell you later," he replied. He expressed his gratitude "that the church had the good sense to elect you. Now let's see if they have the good sense to assign you to Nashville."

I was assigned to Nashville, and our home was three miles from the prison. Bill and I were neighbors! Frequent visits were now possible. Though my title changed, and my first name was customarily changed to "Bishop," I remained "Ken" to Bill. My times with Bill persistently reminded me, amid the challenges and conflicts of the episcopacy, that I had choices to laugh or cry and that the One who "lives on death row" will never leave me alone. Bill's authenticity and unconditional acceptance frequently challenged my temptations to hide personal vulnerability and insecurities behind the episcopal office and to be seduced by its pomp and praise.

I learned how Bill made the telephone call after my election. The supervisor on duty owed Bill a special debt. When a riot broke out in the old prison facility approximately eight years earlier, the officer, now the supervisor, was taken hostage. Bill helped mediate the conflict and avoid further violence. The supervisor credited Bill with saving his life. When the news of my election came, he suggested Bill make the call.

A New Trial for Bill

Bill's twenty-year pleas finally came to fruition in 1998 when he was granted a new trial set for February 1999. The case received extensive media coverage. Bill had become a symbol of the death penalty controversy. Current and aspiring politicians used the case to advance their ambitions. Death penalty advocates bemoaned the slowness of the state in executing death row inmates and attributed the delays to "liberal judges" who were "soft on crime." A petition circulated for the removal of the judge who granted Bill's new trial. "Letters to the Editor" appeared in local newspapers supporting executions.

After several days of testimony and arguments, the case went to the jury. We anxiously awaited the verdict. Guilty of murder in the first degree. Bill's attorneys requested that Sheri and I travel quickly to Memphis to testify in the sentencing phase.

We arrived in the crowded courtroom for the start of the testimony. Bill was seated at the defendants' table with the attorneys and co-defendant. We took seats behind him and beside his cousin, Doris. She had been present throughout the trial. Across the aisle sat several family members of the victim. We listened intently as the prosecuting attorney portrayed Bill as a ruthless murderer who deserved no mercy.

Following the testimony of Bill's cousin, Sheri was called to the stand. She carried with her a box containing all the letters she received from Bill over the previous seventeen years. She was nervous but poised as the attorney questioned her about her friendship with Bill. "How would you describe your relationship with Mr. Groseclose?" he asked. "He is like an adopted uncle. He has given me advice and encouragement. I have learned a lot from him," Sheri remarked.

When asked what she had learned, she replied, "You can't ultimately judge people by stereotypes. You must get to know them as people, and those on death row are people, too." She shared that the only thing Bill ever asked for was the color of her room because he wanted his paintings for her to match the décor. She gave the jurors a glimpse of his humor by recounting how he arranged with her mom and dad to put rice in the car at her wedding with a note attached, "I just wanted to let you know I was here. Sorry I couldn't stay for the reception, Bill."

It was my turn to take the stand. I recounted my experiences, including his call when I was elected a bishop, soliciting smiles from a few jurors. I emphasized his contribution to our family and the other prisoners. When asked if he had value to me, I declared, "He certainly does, and he has value to God." The prosecutor rose and objected to my mention of God, and the judge sustained the objection. The irony was that the court administered the oath to me "so help me God," but I could not refer to God in referencing Bill's value.

Other witnesses for Bill included the former warden and other correctional officers. They described him as a model prisoner who was like a staff member. Two men living on death row testified about Bill's ministry to them. Both had received their GEDs under his tutorage, and they explained how their lives had been "turned around" by their friendship with him. One shared the story of Bill painting pictures of animals and Smurfs, contributing them anonymously to a local children's home as Christmas gifts.

The sentencing verdict was returned in late afternoon. Tears flowed as the sentence was read, "Life in prison." His life had been spared. His attorneys affirmed that our testimony had made a significant difference in humanizing Bill and countering the image as portrayed by the prosecution.

Bill was returned to Nashville and released into the general prison population. For the first time in twenty-one years, he could lie in the grass on the prison grounds. Now he could hear the birds sing and look for four-leaf clovers. He delighted in rabbits playing outside the prison fence and kept watch over a family of sparrows nesting in a nearby tree.

He was soon mysteriously reclassified and transferred to a facility in a remote area of West Tennessee. His attorneys speculated that political pressure was applied to the Department of Correction to make his conditions as harsh as possible. His new location made visits with his cousin impossible and very difficult for friends. On my first visit to his new location, I found him discouraged but still hopeful. The circumstances were tragic, but he still managed to laugh. He refused to let his mind be imprisoned. He repeated a previous affirmation of his: "They've got my body, but they can't have my mind." Although hundreds of miles separated us over the next fifteen years and visits were now infrequent, our friendship continued.

Early in 2015, Bill became ill. Medical care in the prison is minimal, at best. Severe and recurring pain was being treated with Tylenol and aspirin. After weeks of not hearing from him and since we now lived in South Carolina, I asked a pastor colleague to visit Bill. He learned that Bill had been transferred to the prison medical facility in Nashville and was in the late stages of liver disease. He was dying! Sheri and I arranged a visit.

Seeing Bill with yellowing skin, his body now frail and weak, his once sparkling blue eyes now discolored and distant, and his firm voice reduced to a whisper was almost overwhelming. Adding to the dismay was his physical surroundings—drab walls, concrete and steel, no flowers or plants, no beauty, only starkness. Medical staff seemed calloused and cold. Though barely able to sit up in bed, his right ankle was cuffed to the bed frame. Everything communicated isolation, aloneness, apathy, harshness, death, evil, barbarism!

Our final visit a couple of weeks later was especially painful. As we held Bill's hands, I asked if there was anything Sheri and I could do for him. He asked us to notify his cousin. Then he requested that we attempt to find his son, Brian, whom he had not seen in thirty-eight years. He gave us his son's adopted last name[32] but had no contact information. He added that if we located him, simply let him know that his dad would be pleased to see him, though he would understand if he preferred otherwise.

With the use of technology, Sheri located Brian. She sent a message explaining the situation and invited him to respond if inclined to do so. She provided our telephone numbers, and within a very short time, the son called. Yes, he wanted to visit his dad! He had recently gotten involved through his church in visiting a prison and felt a nudge to connect with his dad, even though other family members advised otherwise.

Time was short, so I immediately called the prison chaplain, who made special arrangements for Brian to visit the next day. Amid the drabness, starkness, and barbarism of a prison hospital, a joyous reunion happened. Forgiveness and reconciliation occurred. Bill could die in peace, and his son could live more freely into the future.

Death followed within a couple of days. Bill had

---

[32] The son was the product of Bill's first wife, not the wife that had been murdered. He was adopted by his stepfather, hence the change in name from Groseclose.

requested that I conduct the funeral and that he be buried beside his mother in Saltville, Virginia. Appropriate arrangements were made, and on a sunny September morning, we gathered on a hillside to lay to rest William Groseclose. Present were Bill's cousin and a couple of her family members; Sheri and her husband, John; Cari Willis, a former student who knew of my friendship with Bill; and Bill's son and his wife. Two representatives from the funeral home stood by. Included in the service were appropriate scriptures and brief comments by me. I shared the memory of the first visit Sheri and I made in 1982 and concluded by referring to Bill's etching on the chalkboard and the words: "Jesus, our brother, lives on death row." Not only was Jesus, our brother, portrayed in the image on the chalkboard, but he also showed up in the one who sat across the table from us. I experienced the risen Christ in Bill many times over the years.

We shared memories of Bill and gratitude for the gifts he had brought to our lives. Without knowing his father requested we sing "Amazing Grace" at his funeral, Brian asked if he might sing "Amazing Grace" as a gift to his father. There amid the rolling hills, the son of a man who spent almost four decades in prison, twenty of them on death row, echoed across the tranquil valley:

Amazing grace!
How sweet the sound that saves a wretch like me!
I once was lost, but now am found;
Was blind, but now I see.

Through many dangers, toils, and snares,
I have already come;
'tis grace hath brought me safe thus far,
And grace will lead me home.

Tennessee's prisons may have confined Bill's body, but his influence extended far beyond those concrete and steel walls. Activists for criminal justice reform found in him inspiration and insight. Fellow prisoners' lives were transformed, and many correction officers charged with restricting him testified to his positive impact. His friendship radically shifted the margins of my theological perspectives and practices as a pastor, bishop, and seminary professor.

Teaching a New Generation of Pastors and Church Leaders

I had long been aware that Vanderbilt Divinity School offered a course on restorative justice and prisons taught by Harmon Wray. Harmon was part of the Southern Prison Coalition and a close friend of Bill Groseclose and me. Shortly after joining the Duke Divinity School faculty in 2004, I invited Harmon for a visit and an informal conversation with selected faculty members about his Vanderbilt course. Little interest was expressed, but a seed was planted.

Three years later, I presented a formal course proposal to the administration and faculty. It was enthusiastically approved. The faculty had been emphasizing that all courses include an identified practicum in the requirements, and my proposal required that several class sessions be held inside the federal prison with inmates participating in the discussions.

Cari Willis, a student, had completed a field placement in the hospice unit at the federal prison in Butner, North Carolina. Her passion for prison ministry was infectious. She developed a trusting relationship with the warden and was eager to help arrange classes inside the prison. Her previous management experience in the corporate world uniquely equipped her to assist in the course logistics, and her pastoral and theological astuteness and sensitivity became invaluable resources.

New Testament scholar Douglas Campbell agreed to be the guest lecturer for sessions focusing on biblical/theological foundations for restorative justice and prison ministry. He shared how his own relationship with persons living in prison influenced his understanding of Paul's letters, many of which were written from prison. Douglas's expertise in the Pauline concept of justification as restorative rather than juridical formed the theological grounding and vision for the course.

The course was first offered in 2009 with the optimum of twelve students enrolled. Establishing relationships with correctional officers, men living in prison, and the chaplain were part of the curriculum. Students participated in worship services, listened to the stories and insights of the incarcerated men, read literature on criminal justice, and wrote about their experiences. The course concluded with a worship service, which included acts of commitment to ministry with those who live behind bars.

An early experience happened in a Sunday afternoon worship service conducted by one of the chaplains. After a young inmate in the facility led us in singing, the chaplain read the story of the "Prodigal Son" (Luke 15:11-24). He asked us to put ourselves in the story since we all are persons separated from our true selves and from God. He then enacted the response of the father. An incarcerated man selected to play the prodigal son walked toward the chaplain. The chaplain removed his suit coat and gently placed it on the young man's shoulder. Placing a ring on his finger, he declared with glee, "My son is home!" The chaplain then violated prison rules by reaching out and affectionately embracing the "young prodigal." Behind the prison wall, a familiar story from the Bible became a lived reality.

One poignant event that semester was the memorial service for the men who had died during the year. The Butner facility includes a hospital to which all seriously ill federal prisoners east of the Mississippi River are brought. Those of us from the seminary joined with the warden, correctional officers, the confined men, and a few family members to remember and memorialize those who had died during the preceding twelve months. Many had died alone, cut off from family.

Using Isaiah 40 as my chosen text, I spoke of prison as a form of exile into which God enters to bring comfort, forgiveness, and reconciliation. I affirmed that those who were taken into exile assumed God had forsaken them, and yet God assured them, "I have created you; I know you by name; I have redeemed you; you are mine."

Following the sermon, the warden called the name of each deceased man. As the name was called, an inmate rose with a lighted candle to represent the life and witness of the one who had died. Reverence, solemnity, and tears filled the atmosphere. God entered exile again!

In the evaluations at the end of the semester, students described the course as informative and transformative. The course was firmly incorporated into the seminary curriculum. When I retired from Duke after teaching the class for two semesters, Douglas Campbell assumed responsibility for the course, with Cari Willis as preceptor. He now oversees a certificate program in prison studies at Duke Divinity School and is co-director of the Prison Engagement Initiative at the university's Kenan Institute for Ethics. He has taken the course far beyond its original content and impact.

The far-reaching impact on students remains largely unknown. Some have become prison chaplains; others have done additional academic studies and research and now teach in colleges and universities. Many of those now serving as pastors of congregations include those living in prisons and jails and their families as integral to their ministries. Cari Willis devotes full-time to initiating and nurturing friendships with men facing execution in states across the nation, witnessing their deaths at the hand of the state. Her personal stories and witness to the humanity of those living on "the row" powerfully embodies and proclaims the Christian gospel. Indeed, she bears witness to Bill Groseclose's declaration: "Jesus, our brother, lives on death row!"

Conclusion

That one sentence in a speech delivered by a judge at an annual conference session in 1966 set me on an unexpected ministry path: "Pastors should be as familiar with the inside of the local jails and prisons as they are the local hospitals." While I may never have fully embraced the scope of the challenge, the people I encountered while traveling that path have enriched and shaped my life in profound ways. Here are a few perspectives gained from involvement with those who live and work among those marginalized by the criminal justice system:

- Prisons and jails are a consequence and a microcosm of the systemic challenges confronting our society, including racism, economic disparity, classism, inadequate educational and mental health systems, political dysfunction, and the theology of retributive justice and redemptive violence.

- People in jails and prisons in our communities are no less valued by God than people who occupy the pulpits and pews in churches.

- We do not *take* God to those who live in prison; we *encounter* God through them.

- Built on retribution and punishment, the current criminal justice system is ineffective and counterproductive.

- Prisons and jails are occupied predominantly by the poor and ethnic minorities, reflecting the injustice within our so-called "justice" system.

- Families of the incarcerated are isolated within their communities and need the attention of the church.

- Advocacy and programs are most effective when they emerge from personal relationships with those on whose behalf they are directed.

- The death penalty reflects and exacerbates the myth of redemptive violence and thereby increases suffering and vengeance.

- Pastors and congregations who embody the Christian gospel have the potential to transform the current criminal justice system from a system of retribution to a system of reconciliation and transformation.

CHAPTER EIGHT

Dementia and Diminishment: Gifts from the Forgetting and the Forgotten

We Become "The Other"

The marginalized most frequently are viewed as "the other." Relationships with them are optional, requiring intentionality in entering their world. I have long been among the privileged insiders with choices in relationships with "the others." But in 2009, the margins shifted again. "The other" became *us*! Disease and the inexorable changes wrought by the aging process pushed Linda and me to the margins.

Subtle changes in Linda's behavior became increasingly pronounced. Errors in bookkeeping, getting lost while driving, forgetting important appointments, and difficulty choosing from a restaurant menu morphed into more risky behaviors and emotions, dramatically evident when she failed the driver's license renewal test.

On a cold, dreary, rainy November day in 2009, we sat in the doctor's office at Duke Medical Center to hear the results of Linda's cognitive evaluation. With sadness and empathy, the doctor announced, "Frontotemporal Dementia." Every aspect of our lives was about to change. We were entering the world of the forgetting and the forgotten.[33]

Being among those experiencing diminished capacities, narrowing circles of relationships, and increasing dependency presents special challenges and opportunities. The challenges are especially pronounced in a society that prioritizes youthful vigor, intellectual acumen, personal independence, and endless productivity. Critical questions arise: What is our fundamental purpose/calling? What is the source of our identity and worth? Where do we belong? What can we contribute?

After a presentation in which I shared about my journey with Linda, a participant asked, "What did you learn from your experiences with Linda that might help you face your own future frailty?" What follows are stories from our journey in the world of the frail, the forgetting, and the forgotten, which help me live toward my own approaching frailty.

A World of Stigma and Loss

After receiving the diagnosis, Linda and I drove home in silence. I reached over to clasp her hand. The windshield wipers worked rapidly to keep the falling rain from obscuring the view ahead as I fought back tears for what lay ahead for us. The silence was broken by Linda pleading,

---

[33] The book, *Ministry with the Forgotten: Dementia Through a Spiritual Lens* (Abingdon Press, 2019), is a personal and theological reflection on my experiences with Linda and others who live with dementia.

"Please don't tell anyone. I don't want people to know."

Of course, people close to us already knew. They had noticed the changes, especially our daughters. "We must tell Sheri and Sandra. They are waiting to hear the results of our appointment with the doctor," I countered as gently as possible. "It's nothing to be ashamed of, and we need their support."

"I'm so embarrassed, I don't want people to know," she protested. But upon arriving at home, we placed the call. Their response was predictable: Assurances of love and support! "We love you, and we're in this together, Mom," was the clear message. I felt a surprising sense of relief amid the sadness and fear. Now, there was an explanation for the irritating behavior I had interpreted as inattentiveness, hostility, selfishness, or indifference. Now I realized it wasn't that she was trying to give me a bad time; she was *having* a bad time!

Linda's embarrassment and our shared fear reflect the negative stigma associated with frailty and dementia. From a very early age, we fear growing old. On the eve of my grandson Michael's fifth birthday, he said, "Pawpaw, I don't want to be five." "Michael, why do you want to stay four years old?" I asked. "I don't want to get old like you!" he retorted. I was only sixty-five at the time! But he knew I was having trouble matching his energy. He noticed the wrinkles and dark blotches on my skin. My hair had fallen out, my vision required corrective lenses, and he knew I had just undergone a surgical procedure. Growing old means loss.

The loss of cognitive ability is the most dreaded and degraded. I've said it myself, "I'd rather lose my life than lose my mind." Among the most frequent laments of people with dementia are these: "I'm dumb and stupid!" "I can't do anything!" "I don't belong anywhere!" "I'd rather be dead than live like this."

Dementia diseases remove filters, often resulting in inappropriate behaviors, and people in the early stages are aware of those behaviors. They embarrass themselves and those around them in social situations. The awareness of those behaviors intensifies self-loathing, reinforces negative stigmatization, and promotes social isolation.

Linda stopped participating in church activities following an incident in worship. About ten minutes into the preacher's sermon, she blurted out within hearing distance, "When is he going to stop?" I sank uncomfortably in the pew as I put my finger to my lips, "Shhhh!" After the service, I jokingly remarked, "She was only expressing what others were thinking." One of my daughters snapped, "No, she was only saying what she's wanted to say all those years as she listened to your sermons."

Humor helped defuse the tension, but it didn't eliminate the embarrassment, especially for Linda. The incident reinforced the stigma and Linda's isolation. It also increased my determination to help churches become more dementia-friendly and welcoming of those whose inappropriate behavior manifests a need for acceptance and inclusion rather than judgment and exclusion.

The causes of stigmatization and fear lie far deeper than lost inhibitions and embarrassing incidents. Losses multiply as diseases of the brain progressively strip away valued memories, abilities, and relationships. The very self, the essence of personhood, is at stake. In our society, lost capacities mean lost self-worth and identity. I am what I know, what I produce, what I achieve, what I look like, and what I own. We have bought into the Cartesian illusion, "I think; therefore, I am!" Further, we worship the false gods of individualism, personal autonomy, and self-sufficiency. Brain diseases strip us of those illusions. Progressively, inexorably, dementia erases capacities—memory, reason, and control, even of basic bodily functions. Autonomy gives way to dependency, and eventually, control of elemental body functions may be lost.

"I can't do anything right. I'm losing myself," Linda declared about midway into her disease. Aware of the changes taking place in her brain, she was understandably scared. Linda knew more losses loomed. She enjoyed entertaining, cooking, decorating, sewing, and keeping the house orderly and welcoming. Cooking went by the wayside. Sewing requires multiple steps, which she could no longer follow. Dressing involves sequencing, and she couldn't decide whether shoes or slacks go on first. Eventually, her brain couldn't tell her how to put one foot in front of the other or move a spoon from the plate to her mouth.

Gone were the capacities to make decisions, learn new skills, engage in activities, and speak coherent words. Family members and lifelong friends became strangers.

After a visit with Sheri, her firstborn, Linda looked at me and asked, "Who was that? She sure was nice!" Holding back tears, I said, "That was Sheri, our daughter. She loves you!" Linda didn't know her name or history. But knowing she was loved was more important than recalling a name. Though Linda may have forgotten who she was and had lost valued capacities, her fundamental identity and worth remained.

Who am I When I Forget Who I am?

Midway in the progression of Linda's disease, we sat around a table with a nurse practitioner to hear the results of her latest cognitive test. More memory loss and troubling behavioral changes required another medical evaluation. With the report in hand, the practitioner looked at me and reported that Linda had scored zero on the Mini-Mental Status Examination (MMSE). Still looking at me, she said, "Linda is not the person she used to be." She proceeded to name current and potential deficiencies, never acknowledging Linda's presence. A beloved wife and mother had been reduced to a zero on a medical test.

Turning toward Linda, I saw her agitation. I had seen those looks many times over the last half-century together. Piercing anger in her eyes. Lips pressed together. Deepened furrows in her eyebrows. The practitioner was about to learn something she had missed in her medical training.

Straightening herself in her chair and firmly placing her hands on the table, Linda stared at the unsuspecting practitioner. With the resolve of a mother correcting a child, Linda demanded, "Talk...to....ME!" Suddenly, the one who scored zero on a medical sheet showed up demanding recognition as a person.

"Meet Linda," I said with a mischievous smile. The embarrassed nurse practitioner apologized, and Linda relaxed. Together, Linda and I shared some of our story, though Linda's recollections were limited, her attention waned, and her words were often incoherent. It became clear that Linda was more than a collection of symptoms and losses. She was a person with a story that included relationships, experiences, feelings, longings, and needs accumulated over a lifetime.

My neighbor Tom has visited his wife in the healthcare facility three times a day for almost a decade. Dementia has erased her memories and reduced her capacities to basic biological functions. Tom insists she is aware of his presence, although no signs of recognition appear. Longtime friends and most family members have stopped visiting, insisting that "she is no longer there." Staff describe her as being in "a vegetative state."

To a group of seminary students who questioned why he continued to visit her, Tom tenderly declared, "She's still a person; she's my wife, and I love her." Tom knows that our identity and value lie in our relationships and stories rather than our capacities and symptoms. Dementia and frailty, however, threaten such destructive distortions and idols.

Norma Sessions writes beautifully of her experiences with her husband, Dale, an accomplished pastor and mental health chaplain whose Alzheimer's thrust them into the land of the frail, the forgetting, and the forgotten:[34]

> *I found Dale staring at a plaque he had received in appreciation for his work as a mental health chaplain. He had already lost access to much of his long-term memory and was losing his ability to read. I had no idea what meaning the inscription might still have for him.*
>
> *He finally said, "That says 'Dale Sessions.' It's supposed to be me. But I'm not. I'm supposed to be me but I'm not."*
>
> *It was common to hear statements like this from him during that time. Once when baffled by something I said, he replied, "Well, I know you are a human being, but I am not a human being. I'm just nothing." Heartbreaking to hear, even when his laughter followed.*
>
> *During the months he was making statements about being "nothing," though, he was living otherwise: helping serve communion at the memory care unit; proclaiming "Hallelujah!" throughout the day; lifting spirits in the community dining room with each entrance.*
>
> *And now, after many more changes, Dale still IS: happily greeting neighbors and enthusiastically waving at cars that pass. It is Dale who laughs with surprise when I come back into the room and says, "I know you!" or "Thank you!" or "I love you!" He is still connected to others and to life. Changed and changing. But still Dale.*
>
> *There is continuity amid the changes of this disease: a precious thread of identity that persists despite change and loss. Like the sky's colors that change as the earth*

---

[34] http://imagesreflections.com/2020/08/14/inscription/, Blog of Norma Sessions.

rotates away from the sun—and yet still "sunset" and still beautiful—Dale still IS—and is himself—amid the changes of his disease.

And as he forgets more and more, we remember him. We hold the versions of himself that he may forget, and love the one who is beside us.

Medicine is vital in dealing with disease and frailty, and more research and development are needed, especially in brain diseases. However, medicine does not answer the basic questions of identity, worth, and meaning. We are more than symptoms and losses. We are stories and relationships. Our stories are bound together in community, and we hold one another's identity, value, and memories.

Exile: Where the Forgetting and Forgotten Live

At one stage in Linda's disease, "Take me home" became an obsession, although we *were* home. I wasn't sure what she meant by "home." Was she wanting to go to her childhood home? The home we last occupied? Or was her brain creating a fictitious place? Maybe she had heaven in mind. I sometimes told her, "We're going home," then placed her in the car and drove around for a few minutes. Arriving back where we started, I would announce, "We're home," and she was satisfied. But within an hour, she pleaded again, "Take me home!" It finally became clear that "home" was not a place. "Home" meant safety, security, belonging, and peace. Disease had sent her into the strange, frightening, insecure aloneness of exile.

The metaphor of exile is especially appropriate for those confined in institutions euphemistically called "healthcare" or "memory care" facilities. Inadequately staffed by underpaid and minimally trained workers, many such institutions exacerbate isolation and contribute to a sense of banishment. Entering such an institution is frightening and traumatic for both the resident and the family.

Linda's eighteen months in a memory facility were the most painful period of our ten-year dementia odyssey. During a phase in the disease's progression, she became paranoid and was afraid of me, making it impossible for me to care for her. Wandering, resistance, and restlessness made keeping her safe impossible. The emotional and physical demands of 24/7 care, with its accompanying sleep deprivation, were exacting a toll on the health of us both. Painfully, we decided as a family that we had no choice but to admit her to the nearby memory facility.

The image of her entering the facility haunts me to this day! The director met us at the locked entrance. As I placed her hand into the hand of the waiting staff, Linda said, "I'm scared." These were the last words I heard from her for the unbearable week the facility required us to wait before visiting, giving her time to adapt. Seeing her being led away in fear into an unfamiliar world of strangers released a floodgate of tears. A shy, confused introvert who valued her privacy and modesty entered a world with no privacy and where maintaining dignity depended on the rare sensitivity of others.

The metaphor of exile became a dominant image thereafter. The Biblical stories of the Babylonian captivity in the sixth century B.C.E. moved to the forefront of my reflection. Literature from that period spoke to my troubled spirit. The laments expressed my pain and longing. Psalm 137 poignantly described my feelings: "By the rivers of Babylon—there we sat down and there we wept ... How can we sing the Lord's song in a strange land?" Where can meaning, comfort, and joy be found in this unfamiliar place?

Jeremiah's advice to the Babylonian exiles offered a way forward:

> *Build houses and live in them; plant gardens and eat their produce. Take wives for your sons, and give your daughters in marriage ... but seek the welfare of the city where I have sent you into exile, and pray to the Lord on its behalf, for in its welfare you will find your welfare.*
>
> **Jeremiah 29:5-7**

How does one survive exile? Jeremiah suggests these: engage in useful activity, nurture relationships, and contribute to the health and well-being of the place you now live. Neither Linda nor I chose our new circumstances, but there was meaningful work to be done. There were people surrounding us with whom to relate, including other memory care residents and staff. Our daughter Sandra was now employed as a social worker at the skilled nursing facility of our retirement community. Her knowledge, calm, and intuitive compassion helped us navigate the stormy waters.

I visited Linda two to three times daily, assisting with her care and advocating on her behalf. Residents are viewed predominantly through the medical lens of symptoms, losses, and deficiencies. The overworked staff members have little time to learn their stories, determine unique quirks and needs, and offer assurance, comfort, and guidance. Their efforts are limited to keeping the residents safe, clean, fed, medicated, and physically secure.

I wanted the staff to know Linda as a person with a story and gifts, not as merely another dementia patient to be bathed and controlled. I wrote a three-page letter sharing key points in Linda's story and why she is valued and loved by me and her family. Each staff member was given a copy. Our daughters prepared a chart and placed it over her bed with the heading, "Talk to me about ..." and listing names or events most likely to trigger a connection and response: "Millie, her dog; Crazy Patsy, her friend since college days; daughters, Sheri and Sandra; Emory and Henry, her college." As caregivers tended to her, they could prompt memories, connect with her, and often create a moment of joy.

Our daughters and grandkids visited regularly, occasionally bringing cookies to share with residents and staff. We learned their names and met their families, engaging them in conversation. We participated in planned activities, like hymn singing and occasional entertainment. Linda, however, seldom participated. She remained in her room much of the time and developed few relationships. Mr. Henry, a veteran of World War II, considered her his sister. He sensed her discomfort and unhappiness and often walked her around the hallways. He told the nurses, "If my sister needs me in the night, let me know." A relationship had formed in Babylon.

Another resident, John, shared Linda's diagnosis of frontotemporal dementia and often exhibited difficult behaviors. He and Linda, however, bonded. He often came to her room and fell asleep sitting on her bed. On one visit, I found Linda in John's room. He had been ill for a few days. As I entered the doorway, Linda was leaning over him, caressing his shoulder and forehead, saying, "I want you to feel better. I love you." Two people mourning in lonely exile caring for one another!

Elizabeth had lived in the facility for a short time. Each evening around nine, she entered residents' rooms and woke those sleeping, disturbing the residents and annoying the staff. Upon inquiry, we learned that Elizabeth was a retired nurse. Her disruptive behavior now had an explanation. She was making "her rounds" each evening. This detail of her story provided great insight, so the staff enlisted her help around 9 p.m. to fold towels and clothing and set the table for breakfast. Elizabeth found meaningful activity in exile.

My own sense of meaning grew as life in the memory facility became more familiar and relationships developed. A new role emerged. I was asked to serve as the volunteer chaplain for the people living in a strange and frightening place. I didn't build houses or plant gardens, as Jeremiah advised, but I devoted myself to living out my ordination vows among the exiles.

Ministry in Exile: Presence with the Forgetting and the Forgotten

Admittedly, nursing homes and dementia care facilities received marginal attention during my thirty-two years as a local church pastor. I saw little need to visit those living with dementia. After all, they didn't recognize me. Communication was difficult, if not impossible. Within minutes, they forgot the visit. More pressing matters merited my time. That mistaken notion remains prevalent among pastors and many family members and friends of people living with dementia. During my five years as the volunteer chaplain, I rarely saw a pastor, and many residents never had a visit, even from family members. What a tragedy for both the residents and those who are missing the exceptional gifts of those marginalized by their diseases and frailties.

My ordination to Word, Sacrament, and Order helped shape my journey in the land of the frail, the forgetting, and the forgotten. In my new role as volunteer chaplain, pastoral care occupied an important place in my schedule.

Daily visits with Linda expanded to time with other residents and the staff. Family members shared their concerns and struggles. Staff vented frustration at the long hours and guilt that they couldn't give adequate attention to each resident. I heard stories of abuse and exploitation as Black American nursing assistants were called the "N-word" by White folks whose filters had been destroyed by disease. Family members shared guilt about placing their mom, dad, or spouse in the facility.

The residents, staff, and their families became my parish. It was the most diverse and ecumenical parish I ever served—Catholics, Episcopalians, Baptists, Pentecostals, Lutherans, United Methodists, AMEs, Presbyterians, Jews, and Nones. In this congregation were retired doctors, lawyers, university professors, accountants, homemakers, janitors, nurses, carpenters, cooks, construction workers, business owners, airline pilots, and teachers. Some had great wealth; others had only known poverty. Several nationalities were represented, including Brazil, Italy, Puerto Rico, the Republic of Congo, and Mexico. They were all brought together by a common malady: neurocognitive degeneration.

Here, there were no arguments over abstract doctrines. In this congregation, faith was an experience rather than an abstraction; theology was lived rather than thought. While they took pride in their denominational and faith traditions, they never imposed it on others or claimed superiority. This congregation's relationships prevailed over prescribed rituals, and experience trumped creedal formulations.

Pastoral theologian John Swinton states it succinctly, "The tragedy of people with dementia isn't that they forget; the tragedy is that they are forgotten."[35] Pastors

---

[35] I first heard this statement by John Swinton when he lectured at Pastors' Convocation at Duke Divinity School, October 2015. He has been a formidable influence, especially his book, *Dementia: Living in the Memories of God*, 2012.

and congregations tend to forget the frail altogether or list them among "the homebound." Rarely are they considered essential participants in the congregation's life and ministry. The temptation to reduce those on the margins to "mission projects" is especially strong since their diminishing capacities limit what they can do. But people living with lost capacities *to do* remind us that authentic Christian ministry involves *being* in relationship with the Triune God, creation, and one another.

The essence of being in relationship is mutuality, giving and receiving, serving and being served, loving and being loved. People with reduced capacities are no less contributors to God's presence and mission in the world than those who chair committees, teach Sunday School, sing in the choir, go on mission trips, lead worship, or preach. They are at the center of God's life and mission. As Paul reminds us, "God chose what is foolish in the world to shame the wise; God chose what is weak in the world to shame the strong" (1 Corinthians 1:27), and it is in relationship with "the least of these" that Jesus is known and experienced (Matthew 25:35f).

Mr. Henry adopting Linda as his sister. Linda comforting John in his distress. Jack helping Linda down the hallway. Elizabeth checking on residents and assisting staff. Dale greeting people with "You're good, you're good" and assisting in serving Communion. Mrs. B enthusiastically adding movements while singing "Swing low, sweet chariot." Ann helping to prepare the altar for worship. Jill and Janann holding hands, comforting one another. José exuberantly singing "Kum Bah Yah" in worship. Mack answering questions about the Bible. Doug adding this verse to "Jesus Loves Me": "Jesus loves he who died, heaven's gate to open wide. He will wash away my sin, let this little child come in." These are all disciples of Jesus ministering in exile!

David entered the facility with his wife and daughter during hymn singing. He was a new admission. While he was being moved into his room, I introduced myself to his daughter as the volunteer chaplain. She immediately responded, "We are Jewish, and Dad won't be participating in religious services here." I assured her that sharing in religious activities is entirely voluntary and that we respect everyone's religious traditions. She politely thanked me, but her suspicions were obvious.

Since David's wife and I were in a support group together, I knew some of his story. He was a retired Navy pilot and captain who had commanded a reconnaissance squadron operating off aircraft carriers. He was in mid-stage Alzheimer's with moderate symptoms. His verbal skills and long-term memory remained. He was very present in the moment and outgoing with others. We developed an immediate rapport. He mentioned that I reminded him of a chaplain he had known in the Navy. Occasionally, he would refer to me as "Chap" or "Father."

Initially, he participated in no activities that seemed "religious." Then, one Thursday, he wandered out of his room while the group sang familiar hymns. The director had the participants doing motions with the hymns, and laughter filled the room. David took a chair on the back row and watched, smiling as folks made motions to "He's Got the Whole World in His Hands."

Following the singing each Thursday, I did a brief devotion consisting primarily of a story from the Bible. One devotion focused on the story of Moses' call in Exodus 3:1-7. I said, "I bet lots of you know this story. It's the call of Moses. Anyone want to share something they know about Moses?" Mack, a resident who knows the stories of the Bible better than many preachers, spoke up immediately. "He led the Jews out of Egypt!" Out of the corner of my eye, I saw David smile. I read the story and affirmed that God sees, hears, and knows our suffering and seeks to deliver us.

Following the activity, David remarked, "That was fun! And thank you, Chap, for talking about Moses. He's Jewish, you know, and so am I!" He went on to admit that he hadn't been a "practicing Jew" since his boyhood. I remarked to David that, as a Christian, I share in the Jewish tradition and that Jesus was a Jew!

Each week thereafter, David showed up for the hymn singing and Sunday worship. Stories from the Hebrew scriptures were frequent themes. During Passover, David's wife shared about the Seder meal. Though it's popularly assumed that people with dementia cannot comprehend new information, their senses remain and enable new experiences. What David experienced with delight was acceptance and affirmation of him and his tradition.

On the Sundays we had Communion, I mentioned the connection between the Passover Meal in Judaism and the Eucharist. Though David did not receive the Communion elements, I gave him this blessing, "David, remember God's mighty acts of deliverance."

As David was preparing to be moved by his family to a facility closer to their home, he pulled me aside. "Who would have ever thought that a Protestant chaplain would bring me back to my Jewish roots? Thank you, Chap!" In the land of the forgetting and forgotten, he remembered.

Janann was the youngest resident in the memory facility, having been diagnosed with early-onset Alzheimer's. Her husband, Bill, visited regularly, including Sunday afternoon worship. He admitted to being "a lapsed Catholic" who had little interest in matters of faith—until Janann's diagnosis. New questions and challenges surfaced for which his engineering training and experience offered no guidance. As the weeks passed and our conversations increased in frequency and depth, Bill surprisingly expressed interest in being baptized. I shared that since he had already been baptized as an infant, baptism was unnecessary. That led to a discussion of baptism as God's action in claiming him as a beloved son and never relinquishing that claim.

On "Baptism of Our Lord Sunday," we remembered Jesus' baptism and the voice from the heavens declaring, "This is my Son, the Beloved, with whom I am well pleased" (Matthew 3:37). "That is the message God delivered in our baptism," I declared. "We are beloved sons and daughters of God." I went to each participant, called them by name as I dipped my fingers in the water, made a sign of the cross on the forehead, and said, "(Name), you are a beloved child of God. Remember your baptism and be thankful!"

Seated beside Janann, gently holding her hand, Bill waited reverently for their turn as I made my way around the room. Janann smiled sweetly as I made the sign of the cross on her forehead, called her name, and repeated the words. As my moistened fingers touched Bill's forehead, tears dripped from his eyes, "Bill, you are a beloved child of God. Remember YOUR BAPTISM and be thankful!" A few days later, I received this handwritten note:

Dear "Brother Ken,"

You have facilitated the reawakening of the Lord's spirit in each of us. For this we are eternally grateful.

Cordially,

Bill and Janann

It was Pentecost Sunday. The scripture was from Acts 2, the story of the first Pentecost. As I read, "and there came like the rush of a violent wind," Bobby, who seemed to be asleep, suddenly yelled, "O my Lord!" I paused and remarked, "I bet there were folks at that first Pentecost who responded like you, Bobby!" Upon finishing the reading, I mentioned that the people present were from different nations and spoke different languages. Still, they understood one another. How is that possible? After a brief pause, someone said, "They loved one another."

"Yes! The Spirit descended on them, and the Spirit is Love," I remarked. Residents with diverse cultures and languages were in our gathering. I asked, "José, how do you say 'I love you' in Spanish?" We then turned toward one another and repeated Jose's response. We shared "I love you" in the languages present that day: French, German, Italian, Portuguese, and Shona. We jumbled the words, and some merely mumbled, but we all tried to say, "I love you!"

Barbara's verbal capacity had been reduced to incoherent mumbling. She seldom stood still and had been pacing throughout the service. But during the sharing of "I love you," she came and stood beside me.

"What if you can't speak words? How do we say, 'I love you' without words?" I asked. A resident responded, "Hug!"

I gently put my arm around Barbara, looked her in the eyes, and said, "Barbara, we love you!" Then Pentecost came anew!

With clarity in her voice and joy in her eyes, Barbara haltingly said, "I...love...you!" A spirit of love entered the exile. Hugs and "I love you" removed barriers among staff and residents, those deemed "demented" and those considered "normal," those with frail minds and bodies, and those with capacities intact. No one was marginalized or forgotten as ALL were embraced within the circle of Boundless Love! We "sang the Lord's song in a strange land" of the forgetting and the forgotten.

Worshiping and serving among people with diminished physical and intellectual capacities confirm the value of embedded practices. Though cognitive recall and comprehension may be lost, the body remembers. Cells remember. For instance, the residents exhibited two different postures in receiving the elements during Communion. Catholics, Episcopalians, and Lutherans cupped their hands to *receive* the bread. Baptists and Pentecostals tended to reach to *take* the elements. Hymns, memorized Bible verses, the Lord's Prayer, the Apostles' Creed, and many rituals from the forgotten past often resurfaced during the worship services.

Sharing Holy Communion, remembering our baptism, washing the feet of residents on Maundy Thursday, celebrating Pentecost, praying with and for one another, and celebrating the life of those who have died, being present in times of joy and sorrow—these were among the privileges of being a pastor among the forgetting and the forgotten.

The "Womb of Love"

"Who is Jesus?" Linda asked after a Maundy Thursday service midway through her disease. She was bewildered as we approached the altar to receive Communion. Bewilderment quickly turned to frustration and panic. I stepped beside her, took the wafer, dipped it into the chalice, and placed it on her tongue as the pastor said,

"The body and blood of Christ given for you, Linda." Returning home, she asked, "What was that all about?"

"We were remembering Jesus," I answered. Then came that shocking question from one who had devoted her life to following Jesus and teaching about him to others: "Who is Jesus?" She had forgotten who Jesus was!

Can a person who has forgotten Jesus be a disciple of Jesus? What is the essence of Christian discipleship? Beliefs? Reciting the historic creeds? Cognitively comprehending traditional doctrines? If discipleship is primarily *believing* and intellectually *comprehending* abstract theological concepts and affirmations, those with diminished cognitive abilities are excluded or at least pushed to the margins of Christ's community.

Linda may have forgotten Jesus, but Jesus didn't forget Linda. Jesus came to me through her, even when she didn't know him. In Galatians, Paul invites us to "bear one another's burdens, and in this way, you fulfill the law [way] of Christ" (Galatians 6:2). By caring for one another, we love one another as Christ loves us. By accepting my care for her, Linda was participating in the love of Christ. She helped me see more clearly that Jesus was no less the Son of God and Savior of the world when he was nursing at Mary's breast than when he was hanging on the cross and asking his disciple to take care of his mother.

Within a year of confinement, Linda's physical and cognitive capacities declined. She lost weight. Mobility decreased. Simple hygiene practices required assistance.

More memories faded, and depression deepened. She was placed in hospice care. The precipitous decline continued, requiring she be transferred to skilled nursing or returned home. I asked the nurse practitioner, "How much time do you think she has left?" She responded, "We really can't determine that, but based on the progression of her disease, I would guess she has six months to a year."

With the continuing assistance of hospice and the employment of caregivers, Linda returned home. Having her in the house and being with her around the clock was a welcome gift! Sharing in her daily care and experiencing times of deep connection and fleeting moments of joy ignited a deepened sense of meaning and purpose in my routines. Daughters, sons-in-law, and grandchildren became regular visitors, bringing laughter and joy into our world. Linda petted her little dog, Millie, who again sat beside her on the sofa. Emma and John from Sunday School delivered a weekly meal and kindled memories of "church." Music, including familiar hymns, played softly in the background as I sat beside her bed in the pre-dawn hours each morning.

It happened on my birthday. Linda had been back home only a short time. Daughters Sheri and Sandra, the caregiver, and I were seated in the living room with Linda. We noticed an alertness in Linda's eyes and a smile of apparent recognition and connection. Suddenly, unexpectedly, the confused and forlorn look of dementia disappeared, and a happy, winsome Linda showed up! It was an "awakening," or what neuroscientists call "paradoxical lucidity."[36] She suddenly remembered who we were, recalled grandkids whom she had not known in months, and even talked on the telephone with "Crazy Patsy," her friend for sixty years. It was as though she had awakened after a years' long sleep and reconnected to a world she had forgotten.

Though Linda's awakening only lasted a couple of hours, the experience helped to shape our relationship with her for the duration of the journey. After describing the experience, my friend Karl Netting, an experienced hospital and hospice chaplain, captured the essence of the experience with a memorable image. He remarked, "You are providing Linda a womb of love as she is being birthed into a new world."

"Womb of love" became an inspiring metaphor as our family members, caregivers, and friends journeyed with Linda into the dreaded world of growing dependency and withdrawal. In the process, we also were birthed into a new world where a fleeting smile, a twinkle in the eye, and simple acts of compassion and joy were celebrated.

Linda lived forty-two months after being admitted to hospice and thirty-six months after returning home. During a visit two years after Linda's return home, the nurse expressed surprise that she "is still with us." "What do you think accounts for her exceeding your expectations beyond the six months to a year?" I asked. "She's been loved back to life," she responded.

---

[36] https://www.healthline.com/health/dementia/paradoxical-lucidity.

Linda and the people in the memory care facility wooed and pushed me more deeply into a *lived, relational* faith where acts of caring for one another add to the flow of God's boundless love. Linda's receiving my care was no less a participation in that flow than my giving the care. Routines such as combing her hair, brushing her teeth, caressing her face, and sitting silently beside her became holy. Feeding her chocolate chip ice cream hours before she died took on sacramental significance. In those simple acts with "the least of these," the Jesus Linda had forgotten remembered her and me.

Preparing Pastors and Congregations

How might churches and pastors equip themselves to be present among the frail and the forgetting? Responding to that question led to developing and teaching a course at Lutheran Theological Southern Seminary entitled "Dementia Through a Pastoral Theological Lens." The course was patterned after the one developed at Duke on "Prisons, Restorative Justice, and the Church." Classes were held at the Lutheran retirement community, where students interacted weekly with residents in the memory care unit. The course combined academic scholarship and clinical pastoral education elements with personal and theological reflection components. Colleagues assisted with the class: The Reverend Karen Young, a hospice chaplain; Norma Sessions, a social worker with training and experience in gerontology; and her husband, Dale, a retired mental health chaplain in early to mid-stage

Alzheimer's. Dale's openness regarding his disease and longtime pastoral experience made him an invaluable resource, and Norma's academic training, professional experience, and involvement as a caregiver contributed immeasurably to the class.

A core emphasis throughout the semester's course was this: "The residents in the memory facility are the primary TEACHERS of this class. Learning from them requires that you get into their world and learn their language, their stories, their joys and sorrows, their insights and questions. You will not be taking God *to* them; you will meet God *in* them!" The students provided weekly journal entries with these guiding questions: What did you learn from the residents today? Where did you experience the presence of God? What feelings surfaced within as you spent time with the residents?

"I don't know what to do or what to say" are frequent excuses offered for staying away from people living with dementia. The seminary students learned that the primary gift of ministry is *attentive, non-anxious, and compassionate presence.* But such presence is hard, requiring discipline, patience, and sensitivity.

One semester, a student requested permission to bring her golden retriever to class. Being trained as a therapy dog, Eden became a model of attentive, non-anxious, and compassionate presence. "Watch Eden and the reactions to her," I suggested. "She says nothing, does nothing, but watch the residents' reactions as they look into her eyes, stroke her fur, and sit beside them. Eden is being trained simply to be lovingly, compassionately, and calmly present. So are we! That's what we mean by 'incarnational presence' in which the Spirit is among us."

Expanding the impact of the course to include congregations and laity is a challenge occupying my attention now. I join with colleague Bishop Lawson Bryan and representatives from denominational agencies, especially Discipleship Ministries, in igniting and fostering a movement with caring as a core component of Christian discipleship. Several students from the classes have already become leaders in the efforts of their local congregations and denominations. The efforts are continuing ways I seek to live out my baptismal identity, clergy ordination, and consecration as a bishop as I approach my frail years.

Conclusion

Accepting frailty with its diminished energy, narrowing circle of engagement and influence, and lessened physical and cognitive capacities is the formidable challenge of growing old. The challenge can be overwhelming in our hyper-cognitive, individualistic culture, which places prime value on youthful vigor, personal productivity, ever-expanding influence, and unrelenting self-sufficiency. The aging process represents an inevitable demolishment of such societal idols, resulting in pushing to the margins those considered frail, weak, and incapacitated.

Yet, those living with frailty, especially those with severe cognitive impairment, challenge prevailing assumptions about what it means to be a person of worth and value and the essence of life's meaning. The following are among the gifts I am learning from the frail, the forgetting, and the forgotten:

- Identity and worth lie in our stories and relationships, not in our individual capacities.
- Our identity and worth are held in community: "I am because we are."
- We are stewards, keepers, and nurturers of one another's identity and stories.
- We only lose our memories and our identities if we lose our community.
- Christian discipleship is *being* more than believing and doing.
- We are participants in the Triune God's dance of love, contributors to the flow of love.
- Receiving love is no less a participation in the flow of divine love than giving love.
- Tasks may be burdensome, but no one loved is a burden.
- Jesus was no less the Son of God and Savior of the world while nursing dependently at Mary's breast than when he was hanging on the cross or teaching on the mountainside.
- The church is called to be a community of grace in which the frail, the forgetting, and the forgotten are central to its nature and mission.

Part III

CONCLUSION

CHAPTER NINE
Margins Keep Shifting

Sharing in the Bigger Story

Life begins in total dependency within the restricted confines of the womb, where cells develop and multiply in the complex evolutionary process of becoming a person. Birth bursts the restrictive boundaries and thrusts us into a new world with ever-broadening horizons, expanding margins, widening circles of relationships, and complexifying interdependency. Living involves navigating the always-evolving challenges, ever-present restrictions and limitations, and forever-present opportunities for new insights and experiences. Paradoxically, life entails a continuous adjusting of margins—between being born and dying, of reaching out and withdrawing, of welcoming and excluding, of actively doing and simply being, of giving and receiving, of holding on and letting go.

Reflecting on more than eighty years of living generates cascading waves of mixed emotions. Regrets? Yes! Guilt? Definitely! Accepting grace and forgiveness for mistakes and wrong choices remains a challenge. But the dominant emotions are gratitude, a sense of blessing, and a feeling of awe before the mystery of the intricate web of relationships and experiences that form and define us. We, indeed, are a collection of wonderfully unique, individual stories AND mutual participants in the Transcendent and Infinite Story called LIFE or GOD.

A central theme of my story continues to be the shifting of margins. I bear the scars of being birthed into the restricted world of poverty, regionalism, rigid religion, and the isms of race, class, and sex. Personal autonomy, individualism, White privilege, and capacity-defined personhood are the cultural waters in which I swim. Such cultural waters narrow the margins, create divisions, divide people into "us" and "them," and relegate "the other" to the outskirts of society. All of us get marginalized by one another in such a boundary-creating society as we live in restricted enclaves of self-protection, prejudices, hostility, and defensiveness.

Yet, the bigger Story of which we are part is one of expanding universes, intricately woven webs of interdependency, and stunning breakthroughs in science and technology. The margins of our thinking and perceptions are being shattered. The categories and labels we use to keep distance between ourselves and others who are different collapse when we listen attentively to their stories and share their sufferings, fears, and yearnings. When we push the margins to include "the other," we confront the intersections of our mutual participation in something bigger than ourselves.

We encounter our common humanity and what I call GOD: the universally present power of Love or Grace, which continues to create, liberate, reconcile, unite, and transform the whole creation into an interdependent system of mutual flourishing. Shifting the margins, therefore, is a lifelong—even eternal—process of sharing in the ever-moving flow of Divine Love, or what I referred to earlier as "sharing in the Triune God's dance of love."

Love Keeps Expanding the Margins

The margins of my world painfully shattered on October 3, 2019. Our daughters, sons-in-law, and I gathered around Linda's bed. The one with whom my life had been intertwined in the bond of covenantal love for fifty-eight years was being birthed into a new world. We had journeyed together across the confines of Appalachian poverty and provincialism, racial prejudices and White privilege, rigid religion and exclusiveness, and the frailties and diseases of advancing years. Now our journey together was ending. Our family was left without the presence of the one who had anchored and enhanced our lives in self-giving love. Though we were thankful her long and tumultuous struggle with dementia had ended, tears of grief flowed freely, sometimes erupting into uncontrollable sobs.

Even though expected, the finality of Linda's death was disorienting. A significant part of my life's story ended. For the first time in my seventy-eight years, I now lived alone.

I was a widower. The caregiving role that had dominated life for a decade shifted. It was no longer "Kenneth and Linda," only Kenneth. Having married young, we had grown up together, and her death felt like an amputation. All other changes and transitions felt more like shifts in life's unfolding story. This, however, felt more like an ending to the story.

Yet, with the support of family and friends, continued engagement with others, and the faith assurance that "love never ends," peace and hope emerged amid the loss. The love Linda and I shared through all transitions remains alive. She lives on in God's loving presence, in our memories, and in our very being. Her love birthed and nurtured us into the people we have become and will accompany us into the unknown future.

Love is the thread that holds us together and weaves our stories together with The Story of God's relentless presence and redemptive purposes. It is the power present in all life that seeks to create, liberate, reconcile, and transform ALL creation into what Jesus called the "kingdom of God" and Paul referred to as "the new creation." As participants in The Story of God's reign, there is always more to our stories, and death represents but another shifting of the margins and the opening of new chapters.

A new chapter began for me on November 18, 2023, my eighty-third birthday. Norma Sessions and I entered the covenant of marriage after a friendship born and forged through a common journey with our spouses, both of whom lived for a decade with dementia. As neighbors in a retirement community, we ate meals together, visited one another's homes, worshipped together, and participated in support groups with others traveling dementia's treacherous and often lonely road. Together, we taught, led worship, facilitated groups, and advocated for people living with dementia.

Norma and Dale were present in the final hours of Linda's journey and my resulting grief. Two years later, I was present with Norma as Dale's disease took him from us, and I was honored to lead the memorial service honoring his remarkable life. Love born in friendship amid shared pain, vulnerability, loss, and grief grew in depth and breadth. Companionship ignited joy, joy sparked hope, and hope inspired commitment to live together toward a new future.

Admittedly, getting married at this stage of life is an unexpected turn in my story. After all, aging is accompanied by increased restrictions, decreased options, and narrowed spheres of involvement. Memories of the past far exceed expectations for the future. Yet, love binds the past and the future with the present. We are birthed out of love, sustained by love, and moving toward the goal of being made perfect in love by loving one another as Christ loves us.

The love Norma and I share is an expansion of and tribute to the love we shared with Dale and Linda. The following is the introduction we wrote for our wedding:

Friends, we come together to witness and bless the marriage of Norma Joy Sessions and Kenneth Lee Carder. They enter this sacred covenant after sharing a special friendship formed over a decade of mutual support as they cared for their beloved spouses, Dale and Linda. Their love for one another is an expansion of the love they shared with Dale and Linda, who helped them to mature in love and become who they are today. The covenant into which they enter was established by God who created us for one another and who brings order from chaos, light out of darkness, reconciliation amid brokenness, comfort from sorrow, and life out of death. We celebrate their marriage as a visible sign of the newness of life made possible by God's steadfast and boundless love incarnate in Jesus the Christ, who blessed marriage by his presence at the wedding in Cana of Galilee.

Norma and I are committed to presence and ministry with people on the margins of society, particularly those living with frailty and neurocognitive decline. That is our context as our stories join together as part of God's eternal Story of Love, which continues to create, liberate, restore, reconcile, heal, and transform human hearts, communities, nations, and the entire cosmos.

Jesus Shifts the Margins and Provides a Way Forward

John Swinton is a preeminent pastoral theologian who significantly influenced how I view marginalization. Having spent his professional life among people with cognitive and other disabilities, Swinton does theology through the lens of those society pushes to the periphery but whom God claims as prime recipients and means of

Divine Grace. He writes:

> *It is certainly the case that Jesus sat with the marginalized and it is also true that he offered them friendship, acceptance and a valued place within his coming Kingdom. ... He certainly sat with those whom religious society had excluded and rejected as unclean and unworthy of attention. However, in sitting with such people, Jesus, who was and is God, actually shifted the margins. By shifting the margins with the pushed aside at the center, the religious authorities became the marginalized!* [37]

Where God is preferentially present becomes the center of reality. The Bible clearly declares that God chooses the most vulnerable—"the least of these"—as special recipients and means of grace. Indeed, Jesus so closely identifies with the poor, the sick, the powerless, and the imprisoned that what is done to them is done to him (Matthew 25). Could it be that those of us who separate ourselves from the most vulnerable and despised are the ones away from the center of God's present and coming reign of justice, compassion, generosity, and joy?

Ponder these additional words from John Swinton:

> *Those who thought they were pleasing God with their rituals and laws completely missed the point of what God was up to. They didn't realize that Jesus had moved the margins to a totally different place. Now it was established religion that found itself alienated and stigmatized. Those who thought they knew God continued to assume this to be the case.*

---

[37] John W. Swinton, "Doing Small Things with Extraordinary Love: Congregational Care of People Experiencing Mental Health Problems," ABC Religion and Ethics, October 2014.

But God was with a totally different group of people doing something quite different: offering friendship and acceptance and revealing the Kingdom in and through that friendship. Jesus offered no "technique" or "expertise." He simply gifted time, presence, space, patience and friendship. He befriended the tax collectors and sinners; he befriended the prostitute, the stranger and the stigmatized. He offered relational space and time to people for whom the world (and religion) had no time. In and through his friendships, he gave people back their names. Indeed, he gave them new names: "I no longer call you servants; now I call you friends."[38]

The contemporary world is being violently torn apart by religious, political, economic, racial, ethnic, and ideological divisions. Preoccupation with defending borders, defining boundaries, protecting privilege, and destroying perceived opponents dominate the agendas of political parties, nations, and religions. Fear of lost dominance and control runs deep, resulting in defensive isolation and attack of those deemed "the other." It's a familiar part of the journey from poverty to power, from powerlessness to privilege, from exclusiveness to inclusion. Insecurity feeds rigidity. Fear fuels violence. Certainty removes mystery. Arrogance diminishes awe. Exclusion empowers hate. Marginalization prevents beloved community.

Jesus' practice of shifting the margins provides a way forward. Reflecting on the life, teaching, death, and resurrection of Jesus, the Apostle Paul declared God's vision for creation:

---

[38] Swinton, "Doing Small Things."

So if anyone is in Christ, there is a new creation: everything old has passed away; see, everything has become new! All this is from God, who reconciled us to himself through Christ, and has given us the ministry of reconciliation; that is, in Christ God was reconciling the world to himself ... and entrusting the message of reconciliation to us.

2 Corinthians 5:17-19; see also Colossians 1:15-20

The core message of the Christian Story is that the God who brings this magnificent and mysterious universe into being and sustains it through the power of love became incarnate in Jesus the Christ. The Story enters our stories, infusing our experiences and relationships with the power of love and wooing us to share in God's mission of shifting margins so that ALL are included in the Beloved Community. In this new community, the least and most vulnerable play prominent roles, drawing us toward growth in "the fruit of the Spirit"—love, joy, peace, patience, kindness, generosity, faithfulness, gentleness, and self-control" (Galatians 5:22-23).

The ultimate destiny is the removal of margins so that all dividing walls of hostility will be eradicated, and the oneness and mutual flourishing of the whole creation will be complete. Living now in the light of that final destiny is the character of "the Beloved Community."

The question before us is this: How do we follow the way of Jesus and enter the stories of those outside our margins, those we have pushed aside as "the other"? Where do our stories intersect? Are there parts of their story that connect with our story and The Story? How do we begin to shift the margins so others are included as integral to our stories and contributors to The Story of our oneness with one another and the whole creation?

Common threads running through all our stories are suffering, loss, vulnerability, weakness, fear, dependency, and marginalization. Yet, the tendency in our world of personal autonomy, self-sufficiency, individualism, and hyper-productiveness is to escape suffering, hide from our vulnerability and dependency, and compensate for our fear with dogmatism and control. We defend against our own feelings of isolation and marginalization by marginalizing others. The result is a society that interacts with the world like marbles in a bag, touching one another only on the cold, hard surface.

Still, we long for community! We yearn to belong. We want to be part of something bigger. We hunger for meaning, for purpose, for love. We hold onto dreams of a society where ALL people have inherent worth and are treated with dignity and respect, a world in which barriers and walls crumble and the human family becomes one, a world where all have access to God's table of abundance and justice flows freely. Keeping that dream alive in today's shattered world is hard but necessary. Otherwise, we succumb to despair, which spawns hatred and violence.

A change in how we relate to one another, especially those deemed "the other," is necessary. As I shared earlier, I spent my youth and young adult years hiding my own feelings of marginalization as a product of Appalachian poverty. The old feelings of being an imposter in polite, privileged society continue to dog me. I realize, however, that when I can stop the pretense and come clean about my own struggles, fears, inadequacies, and failures, I am most connected with others, including those who occupy the margins of my life.

In other words, shared suffering touches deeper than trumpeted successes. Vulnerability connects more than invincibility. Honest doubts convince more than hardened certainties. Humble questions move us deeper than dogmatic answers. Acknowledged failures heal while pretended accomplishments stifle growth. Contrite confession softens hearts, while judgmental accusations fortify defensive resistance. Empathetic listening opens doorways into friendship, while argumentative speeches block creative mutuality. Compassionate presence amid suffering sows seeds of love, while calloused absence compounds loneliness. Simple acts of kindness and justice multiply love, while thoughtless neglect and injustice build resentment and diminish goodness.

Conclusion

During a visit with my mother when she was in her nineties, she mournfully recounted our family's poverty. "I feel bad that you kids had it so hard. We couldn't give you what other kids had. I know that was embarrassing for you and made life hard," she said as tears dripped down her wrinkled face. Moving beside her small, frail body, I put my arm around her back, now hunched from osteoporosis, and took hold of her arthritic hand.

Looking into her weak eyes, I said, "Mom, please let that go. You and Dad gave us the most valuable gifts in the world, and I can never adequately repay you. You gave us love! You showed us that love respects all people and treats everyone as important because we are all children of God. No gift can possibly be greater than that! Thank you."

That gift of self-emptying love, present for and with me in the "pawpaw patch" of Appalachian poverty, continues to push beyond the barriers that separate us from ourselves, one another, and creation. That gift is constantly pushing the boundaries of thinking and acting that diminish, divide, and exclude "the other" *toward* a world in which ALL PEOPLE and the WHOLE CREATION reflect the boundless love, justice, truth, beauty, and goodness of the CREATOR.

Made in the USA
Columbia, SC
11 February 2025